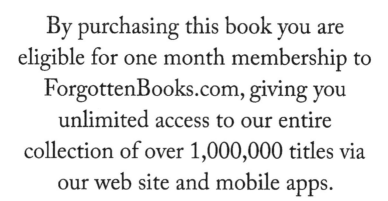

ISBN 978-0-266-19326-5
PIBN 10191717

THE LIFE AND CHARACTER

OF

CAPT. WM. B. ALLEN,

OF LAWRENCE COUNTY, TENN.,

Who fell at the Storming of Monterey, on the 21st of September, 1846.

WITH AN APPENDIX,

CONTAINING A NUMBER OF HIS

ESSAYS AND SPEECHES.

By W. P. ROWLES, Esq.

COLUMBIA, TENN.,
J. J. M'DANIEL, "DEMOCRATIC HERALD" BOOK OFFICE.

1853.

403
.1
.A4R

144384

PREFACE.

THE Sketch of the Life and Character of Capt. WM. B. ALLEN, was undertaken by his devoted friend, Dr. W. P. ROWLES. When he had proceeded in the work nearly to its completion, his progress was arrested by the hand of Death. He was a gentleman of very high literary attainments, and admirably qualified for the task he had assumed. After his death, the subscriber was applied to as a known friend and admirer of Capt. ALLEN, to finish the Sketch so ably begun. He was diffident of his ability to do justice to the subject, but as an evidence of the sincerity with which he cherished the memory of his deceased friend, he did not hesitate to consent.

It is not to be expected that the life of one so young as was Capt. ALLEN, would abound in events of interest, and yet the reader will be surprised to find in these pages so much interesting and instructive materials. The work will commend itself especially to the young men of the country; and by a careful study of the character of Capt. ALLEN, much profit may be derived.

A. O. P. NICHOLSON.

Columbia, Tenn., Nov. 27, 1851.

gone days, would have established the fame, and made the fortune of thousands, seem but common things. Within the life-time of the present generation, lofty forests, where savage men disputed with savage beasts for the supremacy, have been changed into fruitful fields, which afford their cultivators an abundance, and enable them to feed with their surplus, the starving thousands of the old world. The lonely cabbins of solitary hunters, whose inmates were doomed to keep incessant watch over them against the fire-brands of the savages, or inroads of wild beasts, have been replaced by populous cities—the seats of empire, commerce and science, whence the light and heat of civil and religious freedom attract all nations, and warm and enlighten all who approach. The blood-besmeared war-paths of the aborigines are the sites of turnpikes and rail-roads, along which, instead of pinioned bands of doomed victims, pass a busy throng of happy freemen. The limpid rivers and broad lakes, so lately hid in the bosom of tangled forests, are now the delightful thoroughfares of enlightened nations. Instead of the sparse and scattered scores who stood over the wilderness waste, like sentinels to guard its solitude, there have sprung up thousands upon thousands, whose structures, physical and moral, demonstrate the presence and progress of wealth, freedom, science and power. In the midst of such a people, inhabiting such a country, common-place events or common-place men command little attention. But when some hitherto unnoticed youth, a citizen, it may be, of some rural district, unknown and uncared for, by his superior attainments, shining qualities or bold achievements, attracts all eyes, engages all hearts, thrusts himself, or is thrust upon the stage of action, pushes aside and passes

by his seniors, and still rushes forward, leaving them
far behind him, the philosophical student of man wishes
to know the means and methods which have given such
astounding results. Biography is written to gratify this
wish. And perhaps there is no portion of history so rich
in useful, pleasing instruction, as the lives of the good
and wise of our race, especially of our own citizens.—
What patriot does not delight to contemplate the progress through life, of our Washingtons, Franklins, Jeffersons, Clays, Jacksons, Adamses, Polks, and all that
bold band of heroes and statesmen who laid the foundation of our political fabric, or have given it renown by
their talents and virtues? It was not alone the mother
of Washington, or father of Adams who exulted in the
works and worth of their sons. The same joyful emotions they felt as parents, vibrated in the hearts of the
lovers of freedom in all lands. Wherever human speech
and letters are known, in every clime, under every form
of government, freedom has, and will ever have, an altar, on which the God of Liberty finds a daily sacrifice.
Those who now toil around the fields of Marathon,
and look over the dreary landscape from the the cliffs of
Octæ, once the battle-field of liberty, may mourn to behold the change of fruitful fields and populous cities, the
seats of commerce and science, into a vast arena of silent,
desolate sterility; but, surrounded by their ruined cities,
desolate harbors and barren fields, they feel a joy unknown to the oppressors, when they remember that far
over the green wave of the ocean, there is a fruitful land
inhabited by a race of freemen, who delight to emulate
the noble deeds of their departed heroes, whose story
and example serve to rally brave soldiers to the tented
field, whose orations and poems are the examplers held

up to stimulate and guide the progress of Oratory and Song, wherever science is cultivated.

Although the Jew, Egyptian, Assyrian, Persian, Greek and Roman, their empires, and almost the story of their wars, have passed away into the regions of forgetfulness, and many of their marts of commerce and the havens in which their numerous navies rode, have ceased to be the abode of man, the memory of particular individuals, whose talents or virtues commanded the respect and confidence of their contemporaries, continue to be esteemed to this day, and some of their works still retain a conspicuous place in our libraries. The heroes of Homer are the admiration of all readers, who delight themselves with the minute descriptions of the great actions they performed, although the very fields of their achievements, as well as the residence of their chroniclers, are a problem involved in doubt and mists impenetrable. Under what monarch, in what kingdom, Æsop or Homer were born, by what wars or works of art their unknown rulers distinguished themselves, history saith not. Yet their posterity have handed down to us the charming productions of genius and taste, the labors of single, perhaps unknown and friendless men, now the only persons of their race and time, of whose acts and doings any thing is known. While the names of Augustus or Claudius are seldom named or thought of, but with execration, the names of Virgil or Longinus are never named but with affectionate respect and admiration. Such, and so strong is the superior interest felt by mankind in personal narrative.

Among the public men now on the stage of action, and contemporary with the subject of these sheets, few, if any, had better used their opportunities; none entered the great arena of life with fairer hopes of a distinguished career of usefulness. Young as he was, and brief as was his stay on earth, he performed acts and established claims to a distinguished position in the brilliant history of his native State.

WILLIAM BETHEL ALLEN was the eldest son of General Richard H. Allen, and Mary F. (the daughter of William Mayfield, Esq.) He was born in Giles county, Tennessee, on the 16th day of January, 1824, and resided there, with his parents, until he was twelve years of age, when they removed to Lawrence county, where they still remain.

In selecting a teacher to whom he might commit his son, General Allen was fortunate in being able to avail himself of the services of William W. Potter, Esq., then and now, a respectable citizen of Giles county. This able and popular instructor of youth established a school near his present residence, Halidon Hill, in a charming rural situation, in 1839, and has continued it to the present time. Seated on an elevated position, overlooking a large extent of fruitful lands, partly covered with primitive forest trees, and partly under the thrifty culture of his early friends, our student enjoyed excellent opportunities to drink deep from the rich fountains of nature's purity, and to fill his heart with the lofty conceptions which the charming scenery, amidst which he studied, was suited to inspire any one having a spark of genius, or of taste for the sublime and beautiful. There, on the ancient seat of one of the aboriginal lords of the soil, who, having finished his mission among the living, has departed to the spirit-land, leaving to others the enjoyment of the blessings and beauties that surrounded his domicile, young Allen became a student. The same wood-land songs still announce the return of Spring; the same majestic trees give a home and food to the joyous songsters; the same gushing springs and purling rills still glitter in the sun, and spread their refreshing moisture over the plains; the same stars overlook the night, and herald the lapse of time; and still all the splendid grandeur that inspired the Indian with love for his home, the same rich rewards to the faithful cultivator of the soil, make the spot a pleasant abode to his civilized successors.

A large number of the young men of Giles and the adjacent counties, and many from more distant parts, owe their education to Mr. Potter. Being a man of sterling integrity, sound sense and correct morals, combined with pre-eminent tact, talent and taste, for his arduous calling, he, now, in the decline of a long life devoted to the honorable and useful pursuit of starting youth upon their journey of fame and usefulness, has the pleasing satisfaction of seeing around him, many who derived from his counsels and example, their valuable literary attainments, and correct opinions and habits. Among his numerous pupils, few, if any, seem to have deserved or enjoyed more of his sincere regard than young Allen.

After the death of his pupil, the heart of the early friend and teacher grieved as David for Jonathan.— Sympathising as deeply with the bereaved parents in their loss of a son, as dear to him as to them, he had rejoiced as sincerely as they did, at the early promise of usefulness and honorable fruits, from his unseen but anxious efforts to mould his pupil for an eminent position among his peers. He saw his expectations overruled by an afflicting dispensation of Him to whose teachings he bowed himself, and taught others to submit, with reverence. Yet feeling it to be the duty of one standing in his relation to the living and the dead, the venerable teacher, with a hand trembling with age and agitation, and a heart overflowing with grief, wrote a letter of condolence to his bereaved friend. This letter is a model of true tenderness, and genuine eloquence of sorrow. It will favorably introduce to the reader, the future leader of a band of heroes, as an obedient and assiduous schoolboy. It is as follows:—

GILES COUNTY, TENN.,
April 15th, 1847.

Dear General:—However unwilling I may be to add another pang to the accumulated woes visited upon you and your afflicted family, on account of the premature death of your son, Capt. Wm. B. Allen, who fell at the seige of Monterey, yet I cannot let the occasion pass, without violence to my own sense of duty, till I attempt to set forth some of the prominent characteristics and moral qualities of that ill-fated young man. And this I more cheerfully do, on account of the relation in which I stood to him, prior to the conspicuous and commanding attitude he had assumed before the public in the morning of life. It is well known to you that young Allen commenced his preparatory studies for College at Halidon Hill Academy, of which the subscriber was Principal. He had hardly entered the threshhold of the Institution, and taken a cursory and imperfect survey of the great field of science spread out before him, till his soul became fired with a zeal, with an ardour and unyielding determination to reap its rewards and share its blessings, seldom found, and perhaps never excelled, by any youth

of his age. And, sir, I pay him but an ordinary compliment, when I assure you, that his progress was as
rapid as his ardour had been enthusiastic and vehement.
Among the regulations of the Institution, weekly exercises in composition and declamation, were required of
the older and more advanced students; and periodically,
original addresses before the public. In these exercises,
ever prompt and efficient, he soon became the champion
of the school, and the delight of the neighborhood. So
great were his zest and interest in these exhibitions, that
he organized a Debating Club for the mutual benefit of
himself and fellow-students, in which he became, at
once, a bold and leading member. And here I may remark, Wm. B. Allen studied the rudiments, and laid the
foundation of that forcible and thrilling eloquence that
subsequently electrified the multitude, and commanded
the attention of the Tennessee Legislature.

From these youthful beginnings and promising fore-
bodings, we might easily anticipate the succes and distinctions that awaited him on the great theatre of human
action, had he been permitted, by the dispensation of
Providence, to have acted out the part so nobly begun.
But I turn from these recollection's hopes, "sweet and
mournful to the soul," to notice those ennobling traits
that adorned him more than all—I mean the qualities of
the heart. In his kind and amiable deportment, noble
and dignified bearing to his fellow-students; by his respect to his preceptor, as well as to age and experience;
by his modesty and retirement on all appropriate occasions, and bold and prompt exhibitions when circumstances demanded them, he rendered himself not only a
peculiar favorite among his class-mates, but also a valuable companion among the multitude in which he min-

gled. Strictly honest and conscientious in all his motives, he naturally infused this noble and God-like spirit into all his associations. And in riper years, these qualities, so attractive and commanding, did not fail to secure the respect and friendship of all who were fortunate enough to share his acquaintance. If parents are responsible for the implantation of virtues or vices into the breasts of their offspring, the father and mother of William B. Allen may rejoice, even in their tears, conscious of having discharged their duty to their son. But these trophies of integrity and virtue had their origin, not so much in parental discipline and instruction, as in the immutable truths of Revelation. He had often conversed with the subscriber upon the validity, divinity and holy tenor of the Scriptures, and expressed his entire and unequivocal assent to their efficacy and truth, remarking that everything valuable in human institutions was drawn from its sacred precepts. I believe the Gospel, says he, to be the "power of God unto salvation"—and to secure an eternity of happiness hereafter, the injunctions of the Bible must be complied with, be human sacrifices what they might. These convictions, honestly entertained and profoundly cherished, resulted in his spiritual conversion, and accession to the church of his choice.

And in after times, when the partiality of his friends called him to the "political field," a theatre, I believe, little congenial to his heart, or to his spiritual interest; amidst all the strifes and irritations attendant upon a heated canvass, not one word, not one passage, escaped his lips, his friends could wish otherwise, or that did not strictly comport with his religious profession.

After terminating his noviciate at the Academy, he became a member of Nashville University, under the presidency of the learned and venerable Dr. Lindsley.— Here the same devotion to letters, the same untiring industry, the same amiable deportment that characterized his more youthful days, still prompted his manly soul to obtain that distinction among his new literary associates, which, at the close of his collegiate course, he so nobly won. I cannot refrain from adverting in this place, to the high and worthy compliment paid him by the learned Professor Cross, who had been one of his teachers while residing in the Nashville University. In his Annual Address to the Societies in 1847, the Professor, having noticed the death of other Alumni, in a note to his address, pays him a just and honorable compliment.*

"*Since this Address was delivered, intelligence has been received of the sanguinary but successful battle of Monterey.— Among the gallant men that 'stormed this strongly fortified city, none were more distinguished or suffered more, than the Volunteers from Tennessee; and among those that fell, no one has been more lamented than the young, the talented and chivalrous Captain WILLIAM B. ALLEN. This excellent young man graduated in 1844, having been connected with the University three years, during which period he secured the entire confidence and highest esteem of the Faculty and Students.— During the excited canvass that preceded the late Presidential election, (in 1844,) having already acquired considerable reputation for eloquence, he was called upon at a political meeting, according to the usage of the day, to deliver an Address, and, under the excitement of the moment, yielded to the solicitation. Being admonished that party politics were incompatible with his duty to the University, with characteristic ingenuousness, he acknowledged his error and asked forgiveness— thus showing that he knew how to obey, as his patriotic death evinced that during his brief military career, he had learned to command. With this exception—in a young man under such influences, perhaps vitium propius virtutem—he was uniformly the example and advocate of every thing that is lovely and of good report. In a few weeks after he graduated, he was elected

After receiving the distinctions due to his scholarship, and obtaining his diploma, he bid adieu to the lovely and thrilling scenes of College life, and to that Hall that often echoed to his voice, when, in stern debate, he measured strength with his literary brotherhood. He returned to his father's residence, to share the smiles and greetings of fond and doating parents.

But he returned not as many do, with the uncourtly, forbidding air of self-superiority, arising from a consciousness of pecuniary or literary advantages over his less favored associates; but with the same modest, familiar demeanor with which he was wont to meet them on the village-green, or at the humble school-house. He could grasp with equal zest and sincerity, the hand of the whistling mill-boy, the sturdy teamster or the high official functionary. He was permitted to remain at home little longer than to exchange salutations with his friends, before he was summoned to take the field as a candidate for a seat in the Legislature of his native State. Though, by his age, just eligible, his friends so

---

to the Legislature of Tennessee, (from Lawrence County, where he had resided since he was twelve years old,) and where his talents, notwithstanding his youth, placed him among the first and most useful members of that body.

When the call for troops from Tennessee was received, he volunteered, in a company raised and commanded by Captain Alfred S. Alexander, as a private, and proceeded to the banks of the Rio Grande. Captain Alexander having resigned his command at Camargo, young Allen was chosen to succeed him, and in this capacity proceeded with General Taylor to Monterey, where, on the morning of the 21st of September, he was struck by a ball in the breast, as he was advancing with his Company, in the van of the Tennessee Regiment, to storm the First Fort in the North-east corner of the city. Thus fell this noble youth, when he had scarcely yet attained his twenty-third year, and thus early closed his career, which had opened with such bright prospects of usefulness and distinction."

enthusiastically rallied to his support, that he was, after a close contest, elected over an old, well-tried and popular member,* who had acquired the reputation of a most useful and experienced legislator. Of the stand he maintained in the General Assembly, as well as his intellectual exhibitions before that honorable body, I need not speak; these things have been long since portrayed by a hundred pens, and spread out before the world as part of its history. We pass them by, with the solitary remark, that, notwithstanding his youth, he was ranked among the able advocates and talented members of that body. At the close of the session, he again returned to his friends and constituents, receiving at their hands the rich reward of their entire approval of his legislative services. He was not long permitted to remain inactive. New and different duties were about to be imposed upon him. A war had broken out on our Southwestern frontier. The story of his country's wrongs aroused his youthful patriotism, and the thunders of the Mexican cannon summoned him to the battle-field.— Volunteering as a *private* in that brave brotherhood, the Lawrenceburg Blues, he marched with them, little conscious he was taking his last departure from home and kindred. Even in his humble station as a private, his worth became so highly appreciated, gradually augmenting with the distance, that, scarcely had he stepped upon Mexican soil, till his Company called him to command them.† Here, perhaps, the native qualities of his heart

---

* F. Buchanan, Esq., late Speaker of the House of Representatives.

† This Company had been raised and commanded by Col. A. S. Alexander, some years before. When the course of events

shone more conspicuously than in any other situation he had heretofore occupied. By his official grade, en- titled to privileges and preferences over his subordinates, yet he never coveted them; and what is still more prais- worthy, he would never receive them. Disclaiming the one and declining the other, he enjoyed only the com- mon soldier's fare. His tent was the soldier's home, his blanket his covering, his knapsack his pillow. He was honored, in the mean time, by President Polk, with a high official station in the army, but such was the reluc- tance of his heroic band to part with him, that, with his characteristic modesty and fellow-feeling, he declined the proffered distinction, preferring to share the toils and en- dure the hardships of the camp with them. Week after week passed by with restless anxiety, each soldier, like the gallant young chieftan, chaffing at delay, and impa- tient to meet his country's foe. At length the fatal day arrived. The declining sun gilded the distant spires of Monterey. There lay the enemy behind his batteries, forts and entrenchments. Soon the charge was sounded, and soon young Allen was seen, sword in hand—with a sword, the gift of his father, to whom he had vowed it should not be returned dishonored. Placed in the van

---

began to indicate the possibility of war, they had, in response to an Address by the author of these pages, on the 4th of July, 1845, unanimously pledged themselves to march at the first call for Volunteers. Most nobly did they redeem that pledge. The same night the news of the call reached Lawrenceburg, Col Alexander dispatched to Gov. A. V. Brown the tender of their services. Being accepted, they were first in the field, and foremost in the fight. At Monterey, out of fifty-six men on duty, on September 21st, 1846, twenty were put *hors de com- bat.* Of sixty-nine men that were mustered into service, only about forty-four remain; twenty-five have laid down their lives on the altar of freedom and glory.

B

of the field, with firm and undaunted tread he boldly led the way to the deadly breach. But alas! the enemy aim at him—too surely aim—and the chivalrous youth falls! With a convulsive grasp he still holds his sword. Lifting his dying eyes, to survey for the last time his shattered column, he exclaims, "Boys, *I* am dying, but charge the Fort!" Patriotism even in death! equaled only by the intrepid Captain Lawrence, who in the agonies of death, exclaimed "Don't give up the Ship!"

Thus lived and thus died Captain William B. Allen, a young man, when viewed in all the relations of life, who has shed a halo and radiance around his name so bright that the darkness of the tomb cannot hide it from admiration and esteem. Let the youth of our country, whose restless spirits pant to soar beyond and above the ordinary walks of life, learn to imitate the virtues and copy the example of this noble youth.

Honor to his friends and countrymen! his bones are not left to bleach beneath a Mexican sun, or be insulted by the sacrilegious foot of the servile and remorseless Spaniard. No! They now repose in the grove where he spent his childhood. And there they will remain, consecrated by a father's affections, and embalmed in a mother's love!

Your old friend,
W. W. POTTER.

Gen. R. H. ALLEN.

CHAPTER II.

Capt. Allen's attachment to his Preceptor—His removal to the Nashville University—President Lindsley's letter—Allen's Address at Jackson Academy.

THE kindly sentiments of his teacher were fully and warmly reciprocated by young Allen. He ever spoke of Mr. Potter with affectionate respect, conceiving himself to owe that gentleman a large debt of gratitude for the parental solicitude with which his early thoughts were directed. A circumstance that does great honor to both parties, and shows the sincerity of their mutual regard, was, that, according to the straightest sects of their respective creed, they belonged to different political parties. Throughout the heated Presidential canvass of 1840, the warm Gubernatorial contests in '41 and '43, and the still more excited Presidential contest of 1844, the teacher and his pupil, in their several manners, were found in the very foremost front of the opposing parties.

Frequently meeting at the various places of public discussion or elsewhere, their hearts were closely united; they saw, the teacher only his promising pupil, the pupil only his kind and assiduous teacher. Their friendship was more sincere than that between Aristotle and Alexander, and as lasting as that of David and Jonathan. Whilst Allen lived, he looked on his kind-hearted teacher as the friend of his youth, who had spread for him the delightful "feast of reason," and taught him the way to truth, honor and happiness. On him the teacher looked, as Socrates looked on Plato, as "the champion of his school, and the delight of the neighborhood."

No wonder that the venerable man's recollections of such a pupil are "sweet and mournful to his soul." He had hoped from such early blossoms, to see at its maturity, a rich and rare fruit; the more beautiful to him, from the honest labors he had long lavished upon it.— No wonder he tells his weeping father that he still beholds the loved form of his favorite pupil, in spite of the "darkness of the tomb." No confederacy of vice or league of pleasure bound their hearts together. Their friendship was pure and true; it was founded upon mutual esteem, the result of often tried worth. They loved because they knew each other, and their regard was lasting because founded on just conceptions.

From the care of this esteemed teacher, Gen. Allen removed his son to the Nashville University. Here, from a more elivated position, his prospect was wider.— He had, easily and promptly, adapted himself to the circumstances around him at the school of Mr. Potter.— There, by his industrious perseverance in the path of duty, he had made himself the "champion of the school and delight of the neighborhood." This is high praise, and called on him for a further display of his splendid social qualities. Looking around him, he saw a brilliant class of young men assembled from various parts of his native State, and the South-west generally.— Among them a number of ripe scholars, truly devoted to the life of a student. At the head of the College was the Rev. Philip Lindsley, a man grown grey in toiling for the cause in which he is engaged, whose long practice and skill in the estimation of human character, enabled him, very soon, to give to every pupil his appropriate value. Associated with him in the management of this flourishing Institution, were a Faculty of learned men, as well skilled in their several departments as any in the country; furnished the means and having the will to make their College the seat of sound science. Here our young student soon learned the nature and extent of his labors, if he should maintain at Nashville, as at Halidon Hill, a just title to the highest regard of his fellow-students and teachers. That he early resolved to devote all his powers, mental and physical, to fulfil the hopes of his father, and the not less fondly cherished wishes of Mr. Potter. For, although withdrawn from his immediate care, his old teacher did not lose sight of him. He kept a vigilant eye on his progress, and when, at the end of his Collegiate course, he received the honors due to his assiduous studies, he rejoiced to see his fond pupil take his place, with favorable impressions, on the stage of action. The same integrity and urbanity that had distinguished the school-boy, had made him a favorite at College. The ardent devotion to the study of the primary branches of science, which won the esteem of his early teacher, marked his course at College, and was attended with the same results. He secured the esteem of all with whom he was associated. There, as at the Academy of Halidon Hill, he showed that he possessed "superior intellectual abilities." The impression he made while resident at the University, will be better appreciated by the perusal of an extract from a letter of the Rev. President Lindsley to the writer.— He says:

"I can probably add little or nothing of importance to the Biographical sketch of the late Captain William B. Allen, already prepared for publication by his early friend and tutor.* I knew him, chiefly, as a student of the University of Nashville, and more intimately as a member of the Senior Class, during the last year of his College course. In this connexion, his conduct was not only correct, but in the highest degree exemplary and praiseworthy. Uniformly amiable, modest, courteous and respectful in his deportment, he won the esteem and confidence of his associates and teachers, to an extent rarely, if ever, surpassed in similar circumstances. Sincere, honest, ingenuous, noble, brave, generous, he was always and everywhere honored and beloved.—Such, indeed, was the sterling integrity of his character, that few would hesitate to regard it as the fruit of deeprooted religious principle, imbibed under careful parental training by the domestic fireside. He was never known, as I am credibly informed, to manifest the slighest symptom of envy, jealousy, malice, anger, or resentment towards any human being.

He possessed superior intellectual abilities, as well as a vigorous physical constitution; a capacity and a determination to acquire knowledge; and, of course, by diligent study and persevering application, he made rapid progress, and extraordinary proficiency in every department of science and literature taught in the College.

Few young men have ever graduated with brighter prospects, or fairer promise of future eminence or usefulness. As evidence of his worth, and of the estimation in which he was held by those who had witnessed his career from infancy to manhood, it may suffice to say, that in less than a year after graduating, he was chosen

---

* Mr. Potter.

by his neighbors and fellow-citizens, as their Represent-ative in the General Assembly of the State.

Of his subsequent public and official conduct, both civil and military, I leave others, more competent judg-es, to furnish the requisite facts, and to pronounce the appropriate eulogium.

PHILIP LINDSLEY.''

Nashville, Oct. 1847.

Dr. Lindsley has long been placed in close contact with our collegiate population; is endowed with all the qualities of head and heart that qualify him to form a correct estimate of the mental and moral capacity of those who come under his charge. His opinion is, therefore, entitled to implicit reliance. Like Mr. Potter, he bears strong testimony to the high moral and mental capacity and acquirements of his pupil. And if Capt. Allen had left no other means than the recollections of his teachers, from which to delineate his character, the warmest wishes of his best and wisest friends could de-sire nothing more brilliant than the touching eulogy of Mr. Potter, and the no less feeling effusion from the graphic pen of Dr. Lindsley. These were his first and last instructors. Both knew and loved him well.

During his collegiate course, Mr. Allen participated in all the exercises appointed for his grade of students, besides taking a leading part in the collateral means of improvement adopted by the students themselves.— Among those means, the debates and essays on assigned subjects were, as much more suited to his genius and taste, as fruitful in useful results. From a large mass of papers, neatly written and filed by him, a considerable number of his essays, and several of his speeches, * will be presented to the reader, not as specimens of an assiduous student's exercises, as of thought and writing which manifest industrious research, correct taste, and genius of a high order.

During a brief visit to his friends, in the month of October, 1843, the examination at the Jackson Academy, then under the care of Mr. J. W. Dana, came on. His younger brother, Samuel Houston Allen, afterwards his companion-in-arms in the war, was one of Mr. Dana's pupils. That gentleman, with a taste and judgment not often surpassed in one of his years, invited our college student to be present at his examination, and to address the School, its trustees and patrons. From the easy eloquence of his conversation, the learned preceptor rightly judged an address from him would be an agreeable finale to the sifting scrutiny of the closing exercises of the session. The invitation was accepted, and on the next day, the young orator, far from his books and teachers, who might have afforded him some aid, on the 27th day of October, 1843, held a large audience in their seats, after a long sitting, with so much attention and delight, that when he had closed his address, they not only manifested no signs of weariness or haste to be away, but gave repeated utterance of their satisfaction. The substance of his address, hastily recorded in his diary of that date, is as follows:

"LADIES AND GENTLEMEN—I rise to address you under circumstances peculiarly interesting. Indeed, such a scene as we have just witnessed, can never be without

---

* See Appendix for Speeches and Essays.

incalculable interest to all the votaries of learning. To witness the performances of youth contending for the mastery in letters; to observe the rapid and gigantic advancements they have made in the expansion of vigorous intellect, and the acquisition of useful knowledge, can never fail to be an object worthy of attention. Ours is, emphatically, an age of improvement. In the language of Henry Lord Brougham, "the school-master is abroad in the land." Every parent is desirous of giving his children what is termed a liberal education. For this, he is willing to do himself a pecuniary injury.— This will never be a cause of regret with him. The destiny of the youth—the nation's pride and boast—depends upon their proper training, both intellectually **and** morally.

> " 'Tis granted, and no plainer truth appears,
> Our most important are our earliest years;
> The mind, impressible and soft, with ease
> Imbibes and copies what she hears and sees,
> And through life's labyrinth holds fast the clew
> That education gives her, false or true."

Every man, however humble his birth, and limited **his** circumstances, should endeavor, as far as he is able, **to** educate his sons and daughters, and inculcate into their youthful minds sound moral principles. This **is the** teacher's arduous, pleasing duty.

> "Delightful task! to rear the tender thought,
> To teach the young idea how to shoot,
> To pour the fresh instruction o'er the mind,
> To breathe the enlivening spirit, and to fix
> The generous purpose in the breast."

Our object will be, Frst, To encourage parents **to be** more zealous in promoting the cause of education.

Secondly, To stimulate the youth to a manly exertion, and hold out inducements for them to be more vigilant and active in securing those treasures, which are calculated, in time to come, to invest their names with a halo of immortality.

The time has been, when fathers would toil diligently, and labor perseveringly, to accumulate wealth for their children, that they might "roll in luxury and shine in jewels," when little or no attention was paid to the improvement of the mind. Men were then, in the strict sense of the word, utilitarians. Perhaps the times in which they lived required them to act as they did.— Genius was to rise, if it rose at all, in rags. Patrons of learning were few in number. The wealth of the Indies was more dreamed of than an Augustan age of literature. Scarcely did one sickly, glimmering ray of light from the hallowed regions of Parnassus dawn upon the mind. From such a picture, the enlightened mind turns away in disgust.

Men have grown wiser. They are beginning to learn that riches often take wings and fly away. It is now conceded, that the richest legacy man can leave his children, is a good education. Public opinion has been partially changed for the better, but is not yet entirely as it should be. Men are beginning to offer their hoarded treasures in exchange for the treasures of knowledge. Legislative enactments have contributed to a more general diffusion of knowledge, especially among the poorer classes. The system of public schools has for its object noble and well defined purposes. It says to the poor man, send your children to school, and let them be instructed, at least, in the elementary branches of education. For a neglect of this duty or privilege, there is

not the shade of plausible excuse. He may not be able
to give them a liberal education, but he *has* the means
to give them a limited one. Educate them, and they
will be objects worthy of your pride and consolation in
your declining years. Remember, that knowledge, like
virtue, has its own reward; that tyranny and iron-handed
despotism recede before the lights of science. A government can only be permanently based on the virtue
and intelligence of the people. A source of encouragement to the youth is, that the present legislators, whose
views of progress are moulded on the past, are passing
off the stage of action, and their places are to be filled
by others. Our country calls upon the youth to qualify himself, for he will soon be called into her service.—
She never singles out one of illustrious birth or rich in-
heritance, to do her honor. She points to the youth with
merit, with, perhaps, not a single farthing in his pocket:
stamps her signet-seal of confidence on his brow, and
claims him as her own. Wealth commends no one to her
favor. She invites every one, pressingly, to come to her
hallowed altar, and inscribe their names upon the roll of
eternal fame. Before their visions she spreads out her
richest treasures and priceless enjoyments. She points
to them in exultation and delight, and exclaims with
Commodore Perry, "Our sons, they are the property of
our country."

Every parent is conjured by the strongest ties of kindred affection, by the sacred ashes on liberty's altar, by
the shed blood which cements the fair fabric of American independence, by the promptings of weeping humanity, by a spirit of national pride and glory, and by
a love of his offspring, to educate his children, that they
may be competent guardians of our liberties. Educate

the rising generation, and the privileges enjoyed by the present generation will be handed down from father to son, and become perpetual. Educate them, and they will know their rights, and knowing them, will maintain them. Educate them, and they will rise up and bless your memory for it. Educate them, and the unhallowed altars of superstition will crumble into dust, and their places be occupied by those of the living God, and true religion will rule the affections of every heart. What can be an object of more lofty pride to a father, than an intelligent son? This should be sufficient inducement for the son to see that he does not disappoint the just expectations of his parents. He has the means, if he will but use them aright. Let his ambition for literary honor be high; his design, like the great epic poet of modern times, to leave something so written, or done, that after-ages will not willingly, let his memory die.

> Who, that surveys this span of earth we press,
> This speck of life in time's great wilderness,
> This narrow isthmus 'twixt two boundless seas,
> The past, the future, two eternities! —
> Would sully the bright spot, or leave it bare,
> When he might build him a bright temple there?

Is there not a youth listening to me who has commenced building this proud temple? Is there no spark of celestial fire glowing in his bosom? I this day draw aside the veil, and point him to the brilliant beacons blazing from the hill-tops of science, where, he may read emblazoned in inextinguishable characters, the names of men renowned for attainments he may achieve. Who knows but I address a youth, to-day, who is destined to wield the sceptre of government? Perhaps, within these walls is a future Washington, destined to lead our patriotic armies, through a bloody revolution, to victory and conquest, and to preside as Chief Magistrate of this mighty nation? Under this humble roof there may be a Patrick Henry, who will burst forth from his obscurity, astonish the world, and cause the thrones of despots to shake to their very centre, by his native, original, irresistible eloquence. I may be addressing a young Franklin, who is to catch the angry thunderbolt and lay it harmless at his feet. All these glowing anticipations, and yet greater, may be realized by giving their minds the proper direction, now while young. They need but to aspire, qualify themselves, and be the pride and glory of their country.

And *you*, young gentlemen, who have passed from the care of teachers and have began to gain a footing on the great arena of civil action, *you* have an important part to act in this matter. You must rise or fall by your own exertions. A bright and joyous future shines before *you*. Honors and distinctions are at *your* command. Let it be graven on your minds that

> *"*Honor and shame from no condition rise,
> *Act well your part;* there all the honor lies."
>   *   *   *   *   *   *   *
> " *Worth makes the man,* want of it the fellow,
> The rest is all, but leather and prunella."

Let no obstacle discourage you, though it seem as mountain high. You may conclude, as probably some of you have concluded, that, because your parents are poor, you have no claims to literary distinctions. This is not the least discouraging, when we consider that those whose names are most conspicuous in history were born of poor parentage. The rich are apt to be content

with the inglorious ease and luxury their wealth secures
them.   The best and largest contributions to the sum of
human science, have been from those sons of genius who,
in spite of penury and neglect, wrested applause from
envious mediocrity by their indomitable application and
perseverance.   Franklin was a printer's boy, Roger Sher-
man and Bloomfield were shoemakers, Rittenhouse was
a ploughman of Pennsylvania, Ferguson was bred a poor
shepherd's boy, and hundreds of others might be enu-
merated in the same category, yet, where shall we find
names more renowned than these?   How seldom do we
see the sons of wealthy parents excelling in the laudable
pursuit of letters?   I believe it is fortunate for a youth
aspiring to eminent distinction, to be poor ; fortunate for
our country that there are such youths among us.   Because you are poor, young man, be not dejected.   Hold
up your head and look the most affluent in the face, as if
you did not envy his situation.   Let not his farms and
funds impress you with a sense of inferiority.   Let your
sole object be to become men, useful men, of yourselves.
Let your voice, one day, be heard in the Legislative
Halls of your country.   This is a more enviable distinction than any that wealth can afford.   Age, with its form
leaning upon a staff for a support, ceases to be engaged
in the public service.   Youth is destined to take its place.
A youthful Queen now wields the sceptre of England.—
Bavaria, Austria, Prussia and Greece are ruled by youthful princes, and the youngest branch of the house of
Bourbon rules vine-clad France.*   It is rare to see a man
whose head is whitened with age, at the head of affairs.

* Louis Phillip was dethroned after this was written.

What responsible concerns are to be placed in the hands of the youth? The task becomes his vigor of body and mind. Its performance is no less difficult than delightful. To the intrepid youth, even danger has charms. The mind, ever active, is unconscious of satiety. In the language of Beattie. "In the crowded city or howling wilderness; in the cultivated province and solitary isle; in the flowery lawn and on the craggy mountain; in the murmur of the rivulet and in the uproar of the ocean; in the radiance of summer and gloom of winter; in the thunder of heaven and in the whisper of the breeze; he still finds something to arouse or soothe his imagination; to draw forth his affections and employ his understanding."

Young Gentlemen: Childish trinkets must cease to amuse you. You must put on the *toga virilis*. Your age of manhood should inspire with an ambition to play your part with effect and eclat. A thousand hearts will rejoice at your success and renown in life. The man of letters finds a source of real enjoyment in his meditations. He may cull the richest flowers that ever bloomed in Parnassian latitudes.

> For him there's a story in every breeze,
> For him a picture lives in every wave.

Let the example of departed worth cheer and animate you. Let the example of Demosthenes in his silent cave, and on the banks of the noisy sea encourage you. Let Franklin's zeal and success brighten your hopes. Let these names be models for your imitation and you *will* succeed. The student's toils and lucubrations are not to be ended with your active years of life. They afford consolation and delight to declining years.

> Fancy pours
> Afresh, her beauties on his busy thought,
> Her first endearments twining round the soul,
> With all the witchery of ensnaring love.

And, young ladies, *you* should have cultivated minds and literary tastes, also. It is true you are not expected to command our armies or govern our aasemblies, but you have a part to act which requires suitable qualifications. It is not presumable that you will grace the pulpit, or like Fanny Wright, stroll over and scold your country. Such a course, as I conceive, would be derogatory to your sex. You may, like Hannah Moore, Madame de Stael, Mrs. Hemans, Mrs. Sigourney, Miss Sedgwick, Miss Dix, and many others of your sex, engrave your names upon your country's marble tablets, which the finger of time can never efface. But too little attention is paid to female education in this, as in every other country. Woman cannot point with feelings of pride and love to the national institutions devoted to *her* instruction. The foundation stone of such a fabric is not yet taken from the quarry. Yet you ought to, and can do much, to qualify yourselves for a pleasing and useful passage through life.

Pupils of Jackson Academy, your present session has now come to a close. You have been, I trust, diligently engaged, in the improvement of your intellectual faculties, during the past session. You have made an honorable exhibition of your attainments to your parents and guardians. They rejoice at your advancement. You are their pride, if you act well your parts, but their shame and sorrow, if you neglect or abuse your privilegs.— Because your session has expired, think not that your course of study is ended. After you shall have learned

all you can at school, you will have just learned how to
learn.   You should be students all your lives.   Endeav-
or to form the habit of study.   You will then take delight in it.   It was the delights of study which Gibbon
said he would not exchange for all of the wealth of the
Indies.   For the sake of these delights, Petrarch retired into solitude at Vaucluse.   It was this that consoled Bunyan in his dungeon, when writing his inimita-
ble Pilgrim's Progress.   And it is this that will afford
you enjoyments, if you will endeavor to clamber a little
higher up the Hill of Science.   You may then see the
student's land of promise.   Its fields are covered with
fragrant flowers; Hesperian fruits adorn its trees.   It
contains treasures of more value than those of Golconda.
They are reserved for the votaries of science.   Only students can pluck the flowers, taste the fruits, or possess
the wealth of this literary elyseum—none but the patient, untiring student can ever enjoy them.   Your teachers have been endeavoring to point out, and help you on
the way to this promised land.   They have shown you
the channel in which to sail your bark; they have cau-
tioned you of the dangers by the way, and shown you
where, on the one hand, you should avoid the impending rock of Scylla, on the other, the whirlpool of Charybdis.   They have furnished you with a chart and compass,
and rigged your vessel for the voyage.   Now you are to
start alone, on the perilous tour.   You *must* go some-
where.   If you continue straight forward, neither loiter-
ing by the way, nor swerving to either side, you will
safely reach the sunny plains which await your occupancy.   On, then, on to the conquest of a name and
fortune among men.   It is the desire of all hearts, that
you succeed.   Your preceptors desire that you may be-

C

come ornaments to society. Your parents pray that you may be useful to your country. The multitude stand waiting to applaud your success. May you all deserve it, and each of you find it as pleasing in possession, as I feel the prospect of your future is beautiful to me.

I thank you, ladies and gentlemen, for the kindness of your marked attention; and to those of you who have, during the brief space I have occupied your attention, had your hopes excited for some one or more of this interesting band of scholars, I would say that no parent here will rejoice more sincerely at the progress of his child, none more ardently desires the present and eternal honor and happiness of these young persons, than I do. This feeling I trust you will deem sufficient apology for the fervor and freedom with which I have delivered my sentiments before you. Being a youth myself, and finding before me many companions of my early years, I shall deem myself fortunate if I have strengthened the worthy purpose of only one of those so dear to you and to me.'"

This Address was delivered but two years before Mr. Allen took his seat in the General Assemby. There can be no doubt that he reduced the principles which he here inculcated, to practice in his own deportment, as the united testimony of all with whom he associated, proves him to have been remarkably circumspect and courteous, as well as sedulous in his application to business.

CHAPTER III.

The Texas Annexation question—Capt. Allen's first Political
Speech—his Graduating Thesis.

Soon after the delivery of this Address, he returned
to College, where his bold and eloquent speeches, made
in the several Societies, drew him into general notice
and favor. About this time, the situation of Texas had
attracted the attention of several of the European governments. Under the lead of General Houston and other gallant men, chiefly emigrants from the United States,
Texas had, in 1835, burst from her Mexican shackles,
and boldly claimed the place and privileges of an independent nation. Born and baptized in the fire and fury
of the battle-field, the young Republic proudly spread
her victorious flag to the breeze, and came so suddenly
and confidently upon the great arena of nations, that
her claims to independence were scarcely known to exist,
when the trumpet of fame sounded in the ears of the
astonished world, her splendid feats of arms, and reception into the family of nations. After gallantly maintaining her position for nine years, it was ascertained by
her wisest and ablest men, that sinister measures were
being taken to despoil her of the fruits of her toils and
victories. A greedy swarm of foreign emmissaries in-
fested her shores, inviting her to relinquish her freedom,
so dearly and gallantly won, and make herself the colony of good mother Britain, or at least cast from her the
vulgar cap of liberty, and swear allegiance to some

prince of royal blood, who stood ready to become her lord and master. It has been said there were, both among her own, and our citizens, many eminent men inclined to favor these propositions. The powerful protection of more than one great nation of the old world, was offered to secure her from the assaults of her ancient masters, the Mexicans, who, after repeated futile attempts to subdue her, still cherished the wish and purpose to repeat their efforts. Among other schemes, it was proposed by M. Guizot, primier of France, to establish a monarchy, of which Texas should be a part, to maintain the balance of power on this continent. This proposition was justly viewed as a blow at the rising greatness of the United States, and was treated as such by our public functionaries, when the time for action came. It had been solemnly declared in 1808, by President Monroe, that this government would not consent that European policy should be forced upon any part of North America, and this salutary remonstrance had been repeated, from the same high position, by others. It was, and is, the settled feeling of the country. It was, therefore, incumbent on our government, to appear upon the the stage of action. She did appear. But unfortunately for the just fame of some of her prominent citizens, a presidential canvass was at hand, and they availed themselves of the known interest felt by the people, in the fortunes of the gallant young Republic. At the same time, a considerable number of distinguished men, who have assumed the title of philanthropists, and even christians, were loud in their protestations against our interference. Texas, some of them insisted, was a revolted colony. She had not obtained the consent of Mexico to her independence, and was not, therefore,

competent to cede herself away. In reply to these scrupulous and high-minded patriots, it was replied, that
revolution is the inalienable right of all nations, when or
by whomsoever oppressed, and that to require colonies,
driven to revolt by tyranny, to obtain the consent of
their oppressors to a separation, was, at once, impossible, unjust, and at variance with usage. Another considerable class of citizens protested against the annexation of Texas to our Republic, because such annexation
would enlarge the bounds of our sugar and cotton grow-
ing lands, which enlargement, they said, would virtually
favor slavery. These two classes united, and were met
by those who insisted on an extension of the principles
of our constitution, over the largest area, and the greatest number of persons, without regard to the productions or present condition of the people in the new acquisition. The conflict between the two great parties was
conducted with much ardor and consummate ability.—
The ablest writers, and most eloquent orators of this or
any other country, came before the people, and poured
out in copious and constant streams, the treasured accu-
mulations of many years of honorable toils and experience. As became an American citizen, our student
formed an opinion on passing events, and freely expressed
it on all proper occasions. In the early part of the year
1843, as at several former periods, the re-annexation of
Texas to this Republic, was every where, and by every
body, here and in Europe, a common topic of speculation. Shall it be done? was the great question. Although some of our most esteemed and ablest public
men published elaborate arguments for the negative, Mr.
Allen, in the exercise of his free judgment, ranged himself on the side of the affirmative. About this time,

public meetings were held for the discussion of this absorbing question, in every part of the country. Mr. Allen attended one of these assemblies at Nashville. It was addressed by several distinguished gentlemen, long trained, by their duty in high official and professional places, in the art of speaking. The subject addressed itself strongly, to the minds of the people. They called up several speakers, among them Mr. Allen. This was his first attempt on a political question. Had he been called to the defence of a thesis in the hall of his alma mater, against the assaults of a fellow-student, his friends felt sure he would acquit himself with honor.— There, he would be prepared; but they feared the present call should not be responded to by him. They heard the repeated calls for Allen, Allen, Allen, from the eager crowd, with alarm. The subject now to be discussed, was exclusively a popular one. The exercises in College, and the recent origin of the question, they feared had afforded him little, if any means, of obtaining information on a subject so new, vast and exciting. The young student did not participate in the fears of his friends, but did not willingly respond. He had an opinion, decided and firm, and was ready to assign his reasons for adopting that opinion. But he felt all that diffidence so becoming in him. He evidently wished to avoid the present call, but those who had heard of his performances in College, had no doubt he would acquit himself with credit in public. They were not disappointed.— Amidst repeated calls from the vast assembly, he at length arose. The shout that greeted his appearance seemed to awaken all the energies of his manly soul, and attune him to the exalted theme of human liberty, honor and glory. For more than an hour the youthful student,

a mere casual listener to others, held the large assembly
in strict attention, to their seats. He more than met the
wishes of his friends. They heard him with rapture,
and spread his fame in every circle. The news of his
having participated in a political meeting, reached the
sequestered study of his College teachers. Their policy
had been to shut polemics, especially all party discussions, out of their precincts, and to concentrate the entire attention of their pupils upon their own assigned
studies. For the first time—the only instance in his
scholastic life—our student was called to account for an
error. The open, frank and prompt manner in which he
confessed his error, disarmed the sternness of the Faculty, and secured their continued confidence and esteem.
He had given way to the noble impulses of his heart in
responding to the call, but he was not too stubborn or
too proud to acknowledge his error. With this single
exception, his collegiate career was marked by a scrupulous observance of the laws of the Institution, and a constant devotion to his appropriate duties. His graduating
Thesis bears evidences of deep thought, and of a mature
intellectual training, which fully attest the faithfulness
with which he had discharged his duties. Under the
conviction that this-Thesis will be read with pleasure and
profit, it is deemed proper to insert it entire:—

GRADUATING THESIS.

In a country where the people are free and independent, where genius is suffered to grasp at mighty objects,
without limitations to its powers, where rivalry and
competition constitute the basis of excellence in every
department of literary and scientific investigation, the
mind not unfrequently transcends its legitimate bounda-

ries in the majesty of its conceptions, the brilliancy of its exploits, and the rich exuberance of its fancy. The inexhaustible treasures of classical lore, the suitable adaptation of wholesome and beneficent laws, and the inviting official stations which are to be filled by those best qualified to discharge their duties, afford the amplest inducements for the exertion of the young aspirant for fame. The portals of literature are continually open for his reception. The brightest gems that ever emblazoned the chaplet of a Milton, a Bacon and a Locke, may glisten in his own, and the acquisition which Gibbon would not have exchanged for all the wealth of the Indies, may be his. Men of extraordinary capacities of mind and well disciplined intellects, are required to give dignity to the learned professions. The physician must examine and find out the secret causes of disease, and apply the necessary remedy. If he would succed and honor his calling, he must understand his business. The young Sangrados, without qualification, at this age and time, are useless citizens.

The lawyer, with patient reflection and untiring zeal, traces the bloody steps of crime from its source, marks its progress and retrogradation, and pleads, with the soul-stirring eloquence of a Tully, the cause of guilt or innocence. Here is called into requisition the loftiest intellects, the most erudite scholars, and the most consummate skill. Here is a field, though not as pleasant and flowery as some others, which is as extensive as the mind's eye has ever surveyed. Here is an arena, broad and expansive, embracing within its limits *all* the classic grounds of hoary antiquity, and bringing within its sweeping grasp the wisdom of the master-spirits of all ages and of all countries. But a loftier theme than this invites his attention, and inspires his soul. With the eloquence of a renowned orator, animated with the magnitude and thrilling importance of his subject, he may speak of a

" Recovered Paradise to all mankind,"

or in

" Melting tenderness, that blend
With pure and gentle musings, fill the soul,
Commingling with the melody, is borne,
Rapt, and dissolved in ecstacy, to heaven."

exclaim,

"How guiltless blood for guilty man was shed."

These are some of the subjects in which the youth of the country may readily engage. They afford a field for no ordinary speculation, and energy of mind. But, not to their lasting credit, the ambitious for distinctions and notoriety, turn the current of their thoughts into a contrary channel. Unwilling to bask contented in the calm sunshine of happiness, without incurring the misfortune of defeat, their generous hearts beat responsive to a different calling, and they rush headlong and precipitately into its dominions, exposing themselves to the raging tempests and mighty upheavings of popular commotions in sentiment, which distract and agitate our country. Is it because our free institutions are about to be destroyed and patriotism demands his exertion? Is it that our eagle glory is about to depart? If one's country is endangered, her rights invaded, or character aspersed, he should enlist himself in her defence, raise his voice to arouse his countrymen to a sense of their danger, ward off the blows that are directed at her, and point her to a glorious destination. If her territory is invaded by an insulting foe, if the war-whoop echoes along her borders, and a patriotic exertion on his part is necessary to her rescue, he should buckle on his armor of steel, fly to the tented field, and conquer or fall in defending her character from unmerited imputation. He should always stand up in support of his country, or perish nobly at her hallowed shrine. But "to every thing there is a season, and a time to every purpose." There may be a time, when a truce to useless discussions, tinged with a party cast, and surcharged with party rant, may be obtained. There is great danger of men, who suffer their feelings to be enlisted in a cause, like Icarus, soaring too loftily in this strange element, and eventually sharing his fate. Facts are chronicled in history, which tell us the greatest geniuses, and the most enlightened minds, have been prostituted in the rage for political preferment. The malaria is spreading alarmingly fast throughout the extent of our own happy country. It has infused itself into almost every condition and circumstance in life, and society is bleeding freely from the wounds it has inflicted upon her. The flames of faction and dissension are fanned into fury by every passing gale. The fires of a restless ambition burn in the bosom of man. To its merciless prey thousands of noble victims have been offered. Humanity weeps over the innumerable crimes it has perpetrated.— Nor is it the ambition of prosecuting any plan which would redound to the good of the country, but of sowing the seeds of discord in our midst, as prolific as the fabulous dragoon's teeth, producing consequences at last "more terrible than army with banners." The vehicle of communication between different sections of the civilized world, has been employed in the most vicious and nefarious purposes—

"'Tis the prolific press; whose tablet, fraught
By graphic Genius with his painted thought,
Fling forth by millions the prodigious birth,
And in a moment stocks the astonished earth."

That instrument which has illumined by its influence, minds otherwise destined to remain obscurely inactive, and reflected a radiancy of glory around modern inventions, is, we dislike to own, operating deleteriously and injuriously upon the moral condition of the people. It has degenerated into the most flagrant licentiousness and shameful perversion of truth. That, which more than any other agent, assisted the Reformers in freeing themselves and the world from ecclesiastical despotism, and securing to man his legitimate right, has often been used in disseminating contrary doctrines. And can you wonder at it? Have not the blackest crimes that ever disgraced the page of history, been perpetrated ignominiously, in the name of liberty? Has not the most insulting *despotism* civil or ecclesiastical, been brought upon an unsuspecting people under the disguise of *reform?* By declaring themselves the protectors of the people, have not the Mariuses and Cæsars subverted the constitution of their country? Has not immaculate innocence been betrayed by a kiss, and are there not yet Judases in the world? Objects which are designed to enhance man's happiness on earth, has been employed in corrupting his morals and misleading his judgment. In view of such considerations, can any profess an astonishment at the tendency of the press at the present day? It bore such a phasis ere the star of liberty arose to its zenith in

America, and reflected its light back upon the benighted regions of Europe. The spirit that was got up in the last century in the "battle of the books," still lingers around those places where intellectual feats are encouraged. Paying due and becoming respect to the opinions of others, that such hostile array of banners and marshaling 'of subjects in the field where mind combats with mind for the mastery—where intellectual superiority is not the only desideratum—where the desire of one party is to build its fortune and success upon the ruine d reputation of the other, a connection false or true, impresses itself upon our fears, that in the dissemination of knowledge, it also inculcates in the youthful breast immortal principles.

> "The broad corruptive plague
> Breathes from the city to the farthest hut
> That sits serene within the forest shade."

To counteract such a tendency, a very serious and important inquiry might be instituted, whether, with such unrestricted privileges and encouragement to their free exercise, danger to our institutions, at a period not remote, may not be apprehended? In our country, the patriot's home and the home of freedom, no man fears to open the door of his thoughts upon any subject. He dreads no *inquisition*. In every town or village throughout the Union of the States, one or more newspapers or periodical journals is published, commercial, religious, or political. That sectarian religious zealots often overleap the boundary of decent propriety, to say the least, in the mad enthusiasm and rancor of controversy, has been well established. But when we turn our attention for a moment to the great theatre of political action, upon which the noblest spirits and "demigods of fame" have stood erect we forget or lose sight of all boundaries in the stretch of our imaginations. We see men who command respectability and no ordinary talents, and who profess to adhere to the truth at every hazard, forgetting the high responsibility they have assumed—fearlessly and unblushingly clinging to a party for the sake of party—and throwing the broad mantle of oblivion over truth, at a time when she should shine with the greatest brightness and lustre. The subject matter of inquiry is not, what is best for the country, but what is best calculated to advance the interest of the party. With another, I am prepared to assert, that "parties must unquestionably exist in every free country." There will be differences of opinion in regard to principles, and measures, and men; and it is beyond doubt salutary and desirable that discussion should be open, free and fearless. But falsehood, virulence and abuse are not necessary to promote the ends of truth and public welfare, nor the honorable ends of any party. Yet when we consider how little the press, on either hand can be relied upon for accurate statements of facts—what continual stimulants are administered to the prejudices and bad passions of the people—how little of calm and candid discussion of political questions, and what ringing of charges upon mere party watchwords—and what wanton and virulent abuse is continually flung in turn upon every public man in the country; we cannot but regard the influence of the party press as extremely demoralizing. Is this assumption universally and unexceptionably true? Are there not high minded, intelligent men in that department of business who would not maliciously perpetrate a deed derogatory to a man of unimpeachable veracity?. It is highly gratifying to the patriot and casuist to be asssured,

that notwithstanding the various inducements to the contrary, men of pure motives in high places, of incorrupt-
able integrity, and characters impervious to the enven-
omed darts of calumny and detraction, do exist. Yes!
there are those who, though poor indeed, cannot be pur-
chased by all the wealth of Great Britain. Hope still
lingers around us in the gloomiest hour—still emits a
cheering ray when everything is indicative of presaging
distress. When the waves of corruption rise high, and
threaten to submerge the vessel in which is deposited the
"Magna Charta" of the people's rights, we have never
yet been without a Neptune to quell their fury by the
trident of his eloquence, or a hero to still them on the
brink by the cannon roar of war. When the night is
darkest and most obscure, the stars—the "poetry of
heaven"—shine with the brightest effulgence and mag-
nificence. When the shade of a dreadful catastrophe is
spreading over the country everywhere, as the broad
canopy above us, *then* it is that the patriot's virtues and
the chieftain's valor shine forth, dissipating the gloom,
and lighting up with joy the mansions of distress. Although rewards and bribes may dazzle before him in
gorgeous splendor, he never swerves from his purpose, to
be branded like Pausanias and Arnold, with ignominy,
and to deserve the detestation of mankind. In view of
the good it has done and is still doing, can we say with
a consistency that knows no shame, that the press—the
Archimedean lever by which the deep foundations of
tyranny and despotism have been overturned—shall be
conditionally restricted? Further than a corrective of its
abuses, would be an infringement upon constitutonial
rights. Another species of excitement and demagogueism
prevails in our country of no ordinary character and con-

eern. There are not a few aspirants to *fame* in our midst,
who anxiously pant for that notoriety and thundering applause to which the young Ciceros are so justly entitled.
The fires of genius are blazing upon every hill-top,
and the lights are seen afar off. Every man, great or
small, high or low, lights his torch and bears it away in
triumph, to illumine dark and benighted regions. In
every little field are Richmonds more than one,

> "All bluster arm'd with factious license,
> Transform'd at once to politicians;
> Each leather-aproned clown grow wise
> Present his forward face t'advise,
> And tatter'd legislators meet,
> From ev'ry workshop through the street;
> His goose, the tailor finds no use in,
> To patch and turn the constitution;
> The blacksmith comes with sledge and grate,
> To iron-bind the wheels of State."

With a sufficient stock of unblushing impudence and flow
of words, the orator mounts the Bema, cheered and animated by the shouts of his respectable auditory. From
his eagle eye flashes the lightnings of genius, and "thunders of eloquence roll from his lips." He speaks in the
sublimest strains of the sibyl pages of the "Constitution"
and its spirit—of the prime necessity of preserving it in-
violate—and pledges to support it at the peril of his life.
The sensation it produces is electric. The welkin rings
with joyous acclamation and the "constitution forever."
The sound dies away in the distance, and he resumes by
professing an unalterable attachment for the dear people
—that he is descended from a noble line of ancestors,
whose deeds of daring are celebrated in song—and that
regardless of personal emolument and popular favor, his

voice shall be for his country, and nothing but his country; to which the people respond reverently, "amen."——
He summarily considers the whole held of political disputation, weighs with a statesman-like sagacity the important positions assumed pro and con——and submits his
righteous cause to the verdict of a confiding constituency,
believing their decision will be just.   Tremendous and
enthusiastic cheering follows, and the orator, by general
consent, is immediately dubbed the *Crichton* of his age.
A host of others equally valiant, proud and ambitious of
distinction, and vain beyond comparison, armed (in their
own estimation) with the unerring sword of truth, and
protects from the assault of antagonists, by the impenetrable shield of a noble cause, backed with abundant evidence, the testimony of which cannot be invalidated.——
Flowers of evergreen, and glories immortal, are in the
road the young aspirant has discovered in the hallucination of a romantic imagination.   No Utica circumscribes
his vision; no change passes over the spirit of his dreams,
and he stands blameless before the world, although his
principles have assumed a chamelion-like character, and
his positions a contradictory aspect, if the "sine qua
non" of his ambition—the elevation to official dignity—is
obtained.   Like the *Vicar of Bray*, he professes to be governed by a punctilious consistency.   If time and circumstances undergo a partial change in the course of things,
Proteus will be pardoned in altering his views to suit
them.   If by shifting his position, he is found on the
popular side, it would be ungenerous to impugn his motives, for who knows but he is acting under the influence
of serious and deliberrte conviction?   The light of truth
may flash across the understanding prejudiced by the
predilections.   But to say nothing about inconsistencies

and damning heresies, which are very common, it may not be unimportant to observe with what prematurity and precocity of genius, the professed votaries of the country engage in her service. The time has been, when the Madisons, the Jeffersons and the Jays decided constitutional questions with a consciousness of their inability for the task; but now, since improvement in the science of government has been carried to such a solar-height, the young man, whose beard is not yet ripe for the reaper's sickle, undertakes to explain those points with unusual boldness and fearlessness. With a proud consciousness, and stout heart, he meets the ablest champion in debate, and breaks a lance with him in vindication of certain cherished principles. There is no lion in politics he is afraid to beard. With bold words, and Demosthenean emphasis, he succeeds, like David, in vanquishing the Goliath of the adverse faction, if we put credence in his party newspaper organ, and encircles his brow with wreaths, "compared to which the laurels which a Cæsar wore were weeds." So inviting are the prospects, so patriotic the undertaking, and so glorious the results of an early participation in the political controversies of the day, that few, it seems, are such Ulysses as to resist the temptation. Frenzied by an inordinate, though not always laudable ambition, "fools rush in where angels fear to tread." However wicked their purposes, and deep their schemes of tyranny, they always hoist the motto of "Retrenchment and Reform," and "in hoc signo vincit." They profess to be governed entirely by a disinterested patriotism, and abhor every thing that bears the phasis of dissimulation. In every thing connected with the advancement and prosperity of their common country, they are scrupulously and rigidly strict and circumspect—so straight, that like the "Indian's tree, they bend the other way." And, with the confident hope that we will not incur the displeasure or disapprobation of those whose province is unearthly beauty, whose every charm is the magic of enchantment, and whose prime authority is *love*, we beg leave to remark, that notwithstanding the almost inseparable barriers to modesty, and the objections which public opinion interposes, there *have* been, and I had like to have said are yet, not a few would-be *Fanny Wrights* in the world.

We have briefly alluded to the course pursued by the *quasi* politicians of our country, and the motives by which they are in most cases governed. Self aggrandizement seems the secret moving principle to such action. It is not because he loves his country less, but because he loves office more. So omnipotent is this incentive, that many who claim to rank first in the list of uncompromising patriots, would willingly and unhesitatingly sell their very birth-rights for a mess of public favor. To secure office in high repute, they labor, toil, quarrel, fight, bargain, intrigue, and almost any thing else which belongs to the insiduous cunning of the demagogue. Acting according to the jesuitical doctrine, that the end sanctifies the means, they resort to various tricks, and sundry devices, to impose upon the credulity of the honest people whom they profess to love with all their hearts. With what deep solicitude and scrupulous regard should such ill-omened legerdemain and Machiavellism be observed? How vigilant and active should every American citizen be, who is proud of his national existence, in counteracting such evil tendencies? But at the same time, shall we fix a *terminus* to the laudable efforts of the aspiring youth? Shall his vaulting ambition be checked? Is he to stand still and unmoved, when the clouds are gathering thick, with a frightful aspect, over the pillars of State, which augur distruction and ruin? Shall his arm hang nerveless, and his generous bosom cease to give vent to its pent up fire and enthusiasm, when his services are in requisition? No! it's the prerogative of mind, the home of the Deity, to think and act for itself. It owns no superior, it recognises no rule. It's the Prometheus-unbound spirit which tyrants can never control. The prime objection to the effervescence of youthful intellect "foaming up with the spirit of life" is, that it is apt to sound the tocsin of alarm when no danger is nigh—preaches up a crusade when there are no infidels in the city—and converts grave and important concerns into trifling farces. It was probably such flagrant abuses of political license that induced some to affirm, that it was impossible for this country to produce, in the strict sense of the term, a genuine statesmen—that politicians we have many, statesmen none—that we cannot point to them in the exultation of our hearts, and exclaim "here stand the choicest spirits of the age; the greatest wits, the noblest orators, the wisest politicians and the most illustrious patriots. Here they stand whose hands have been raised for their country, whose magical eloquence shook the spheres, whose genius has poured out strains worthy the inspiration of the Gods, whose lives are devoted to the purity of their principles, whose memories were bequeathed to a race grateful for benefits received from their sufferings and their sacrifices." However true such a remark may be in reference to contemporaneous statesmen, it has no foundation in the race of patriots, of whom we are their successors.   They ".filled the measure of their country's glory," and their names will never die.   For them

" There is no vulgar sepulchre; green sods
Are all their monuments; and yet it tells
A nobler history than pillar'd piles,
Or the eternal pyramids.   They need
·No statue or inscription to reveal
Their greatness.   It is round them; and the joy
With which their children tread the hallowed ground
That holds their venerated bones, the peace
That smiles on all they sought for, and the wealth
That clothes the land they rescued,—these though mute—
As feeling ever is when deepest—these
Are monuments more lasting than the fanes
Reared to the kings and demi-gods of old."

Their deeds of daring and matchless valor stand as a tower pointing magnificently to heaven, exciting the envy and admiration of the world.   To perpetuate their memories, there is required no storied urn—no monumental inscription.   That those who have succeeded them in directing the wheels of government, may never cease to emulate their Socratic virtues, that they will not soon forget the obligations they are under to defend the liberties of their country, and that no consideration of selfishness will ever be the cause of an abandonment of those principles for which our fathers fought and bled, is confidently and ardenty hoped.   If the only consolation of the patriot on earth is to be destroyed, if law and order is to be no longer respected, if we are ever constrained to hug the chains of slavery and despair, the *people*, who hold in their hands the sceptre of government, are and ought to be responsible for it.   If a Cataline, in haughty vindictiveness, is beating at the temple gates of liberty, it will be remembered he received his elevation from the hands of the people. If we are ever to be free as the air we breathe, if the sun of greatness is not set in the starless night of despotism, if our brighest hopes and anticipations are to be realized in reference to the continued prosperity of our country, they should be instructed in the principles upon which our institutions are founded. Without such an auxiliary there is no hope. If the elements of corruption, licentiousness and prodigality are sown broad-cast, this is no longer "the land of the free, and home of the brave." If our system of government is once destroyed it can never be re-established. Never! never!

> "A thousand years scarce serve to form a state;
> An hour may lay it in the dust: and when
> Can man its shattered splendor renovate,
> Recall its virtue back, and vanquish Time and Fate?"

But we should never once despair of our country.— There are yet disinterested patriots, who in prosperity or adversity, in storm or in sunshine, will steer the vessel of state proudly and gallantly into the harbor of safety. Cylla and Charybdis will be passed without difficulty, and the ship's crew stand out upon its top with joyous hearts, swelling the triumphant shouts that burst spontaneous from a consciousness of national superiority and glory.

With a cotemporaneous orator, we agree that "if there be any thing which can mingle consolation in the hopes and doubts of the patriot, when about to close his account with time and venture on the realities of eternity, it would be, that in the last, anxious lingering look which marks the boundary of the present and the future, he should behold his national standard, with all its stars and stripes, proclaiming this union of the States one indissoluble and united Confederacy."

CHAPTER IV.

Capt. Allen's standing in College—he commences reading Law
—his general course of reading—his Speech and politics.

MR. ALLEN took his first degree with the entire approbation of the Faculty, and good-will of his fellow-students, as well as his numerous acquaintance in the city
of Nashville. Few young men ever left the University
with an equal reputation. In all the means and methods usually resorted to by students at College, he had
taken a leading part, and on retiring from the scene of
his literary toils, he disrupted many tender ties. The
room and class-mate, the antagonist and teacher, the libraries and apparatus, the rooms and every object around
him were dear, from habitual associations, or use for
years. But his career as a College student was ended,
the books and cabinets, the places and persons with and
from whom he had partaken and derived the rich and
varied intellectual treasures he delighted, must be left
behind. His place at the domestic hearth, so long vacant, awaited his occupancy. The family group in
which he was so marked and loved a figure, were waiting to welcome him back again. The parents who had
watched over his helpless infancy with fondest affection,
who had rejoiced in the dawning promise of his youth,
and had liberally supplied him with the means of improvement, waited impatiently, with the rest of their
family group, to see him, who was their eldest son and
brother, once more take his place in their midst. They

had heard, from rumor, that he had acquitted himself at College, with honor. The sound of his praise was pleasant to the parental and fraternal ear, because it came from the wise and good.

> Praise of the wise and good!—it is a meed
> For which I would long years of toil endure—
> Which many a peril, many a grief, would cure.

On his return home, Mr. Allen carried with him copies of Coke, Blackstone, and other elementary law books. Having made choice of law as a profession, he

tematic study of the standard authors, engaging as a recreation, in rural pursuits of his father's plantation.— His intention was to take an extensive range, and prepare himself by a patient and thorough examination, the basis, progress and present structure of our legal system, for an enlightened and efficient performance of the responsible duties of that honorable and useful profession·

After perusing Blackstone and the Institutes of Justinian, his reflections upon the marked differences, in many important particulars, between the civil and the common law, were remarkably clear and cogent. Several of the rules of evidence and of propriety, in the common law, he condemned, as incompatible with our free institutions. His objections to the celebrated Rule in Shelly's case, were such as would have commanded respectful attention before any of our courts. He was strongly impressed with the superior equity of the doc·

observations to writing. It seems, however, that he subsequently destroyed these essays, as they have not been found among his papers since his death.

In the midst of his favorite avocations, surrounded by friends, from whose society he had so long been separated, he fondly hoped to pursue the course of studies he had entered upon with so much ardor and promise, to their completion. The history of his own country, as well as those of the ancient republics, indicated this course as the highway to distinction and usefulness. In the silence and solitude of his study, he heard the voice of Demosthenes declaiming to the sea, to correct an impediment in his speech; he saw that orator copying the ponderous volumes of his country's best historian, to form his style. He had listened with delight to the vehement eloquence with which the fiery Greek defended the altar of liberty from the desecrations of Philip; and when driven by the persecutions of Atipater from the country he had sought to inspire with his own high conceptions of the worth of freedom, he saw that unrivalled orator, unable to find a refuge on earth, deliver himself into the hands of his gods. Mingled with these exciting events, the story of Roman eloquence and song fell upon his ear, from the voice of Cicero and the pipe of Virgil. Accompanied by the applause of the world, the models of ancient excellence passed in grand review, each imparting a word of encouragement to cheer the student on his way. From such a presence, with the elevating sentiments it inspired, the review of our own Anglo-Saxon annals, the fires of Smithfield and the blood of Charles, he turned to look over the long legends of colonial vassalage and our Revolutionary fields. There he contemplated with awe and reverence, the majestic figures of our fathers. The sword of our Washingtons and Jacksons, the pen of Jefferson and Madison, with their immortal associates, charmed his young heart, and filled his young soul with grand and glorious views of the human mind and its gigantic achievements, when directed by right intentions, aiming at worthy objects. Retrospecting the whole range of past history, in every age and country, he saw that lasting honors, fame and fortune might be attained, only by qualifying himself to become useful to his fellow men. From this grand survey, which he had just completed under the guidance of able teachers, he retired to his chosen pursuit, with a firm resolution to follow in the footsteps of those exalted men, whose history and principles he had thoroughly studied and truly admired.

Looking back over the past, and forward to the future, he firmly resolved to give himself up to honest and laborious cultivation of his mind. The achievements of departed genius and worth gave him energy; the picture of his own future progress inspired him with hope. Having breathed the pure invigorating air of Helicon, and tasted the sweet waters of Castalia, his soul was fired with the wish to know. To stand on the topmost peak of Parnassus, and see the utmost limits of the scientific horizon.

> The wish to know—the endless thirst,
>   Which even by quenching is awak'd,
> And which becomes or bless'd or curs'd
>   As is the fount whereat 'tis slak'd.

Instead of seeking for amusement in the fruitless waste of time, in the frivolous, often equivocal pursuits of young gentlemen of his age and circumstances, he continued to apply himself to the pleasing and profitable study of his profession, and of poetry, history and the natural sciences. His chief attention was given to the learned works of Coke, Bacon, Blackstone and Kent; his hours of recreation to Botany, Geology and Mineralogy, for the pursuit of which the residence of his father was favorably situated. While seriously devoted to these favorite pursuits, he still kept up his social connections with the youth of his vicinity, and carried on, for one of his age, an extensive correspondence with numerous friends in distant places. He also wrote some of the best contributions published in some of the neighboring periodicals. He had scarcely adapted himself to the sequestered situation chosen for the continuation of his studies, when he was summoned from his books to appear before the people as an advocate for his country's rights, against the adverse opinions of some of our own citizens. Rumors were still rife of his successful oratorical performances during his residence in Nashville. The people, and the Congress of Texas, with almost unanimous voices, had repeatedly asked to be admitted into our Union as a State. Our government having acceeded to the demand, the two great parties into which our citizens are divided, either condemned or sanctioned the act, carrying the discussion of the question into every election, even for State offices.

The investigation and discussion of this subject was connected with our claims to the territory of Oregon, and required a minute and extensive acquaintance with the colonial and diplomatic history of several remarkable periods in the career of this country, and those with which it has had intercourse. At the same time, the controversies between the great parties involved other, almost all the great questions of political economy, and national and domestic policy. On the absorbing questions of finance, commerce, internal improvements and the right

construction of the constitution, parties had always existed, but were now more widely sundered and highly
excited than ever before—except, perhaps, during the
last war with England.

With the principles, the acts and doings of these two
great political parties into which our eitzens are separated, it is not here intended to meddle, further than may
be necessary to place the opinions and actions of our subject in a proper point of view.

Mr. Allen, adopting the principles of his father, had
ranged himself on the side of that party to which he belonged.   During the presidential canvass of 1840, his position as a student, did not require, or even permit him
to engage in the contest.   From his quiet, though not
isolated position, at Halidon Hill, he had it in his power
to take a calm, close view of passing events.   He knew
that every citizen, not only had the right to his own opinion on any subject involving the interests of the republic, but the power to give effect to such opinion.   Being
familiar with the history of the Greek and Roman republics, he could readily compare passing events with past
history—the present race of public men with those great
names whose genius, eloquence and patriotism have been
the unsurpassed models of all subsequent times and
countries.   It will be for the reader to infer what judgment the frank and virtuous mind of an intelligent youth,
such as Mr. Allen was, would form of some of the men
who then figured in front of the fiery fray.   Having read
the history of our Revolution and of its orators, statesmen and warriors, and marked which of them, and in
what quality they resembled the great patriots of the ancient republics, the political arena of 1840, with its excited dramatis personæ, presented him a lesson as rich in

useful instruction as the Isthmian games, or Ludi Circen-
ses, to the ancient student of human nature in Greece or
Rome. For, whatever may have been the design of those
public orations, called stump-speeches, the manner in
which and the men by whom they were then and since
conducted, could have been not otherwise useful to the
cause of truth than as mere exhibitions of mental—rather
lingual—gladiatorial skill and cunning. During that
stormy period, no historical fact, however well authenti-
cated, no man's reputation, however well established,
was regarded. Like some hungry hydra, the demon of
party swept this fair land from Maine to Florida, from
the Atlantic to the Pacific. And, like the hydra, its
heads were numerous and indestructible. The very
means used for its destruction opened fresh fountains of
wrath and multiplied its power of mischief. Neither age,
sex, nor services could shield the living, nor the sanctity
of the grave shelter the dead. In its awful, sinuous and
slimy march, all men and all things were forced to assist
its progress, or fall amidst the immense mass of wreck
and ruin that marks its passage. The tenderest ties of
kindred and friendship, the joys of connubial life, and
the very fane of faith, were rent, trampled down and
overturned.

> High towers, fair temples, goodly theatres,
> Strong walls, rich porches, princely palaces,
> Fine streets, brave houses, sacred sepulchres,
> Sure gates, sweet gardens, stately galleries,
> All these, oh party! thou hast turned to dust,
> They're overgrown with black oblivious rust.

Neither the long tried and well established maxims of
political economy, finance or trade, nor the terrible recollections of the ruinous consequences of disregarding

them, arrest the ruin or allay the storm. The voice of reason, the persuasions of truth were drowned in the tremendous clamor. In vain did moderate men seek to check or change the direction of that mighty tornado of passion and prejudice; in vain every appeal to the splendid past, or promising future glory, honor and happiness of the republic! On, on, on, the turbid torrent rolled, regardless of restraint, right, reason, or the ruin that everywhere marked its course.

That the young mind of the true-hearted and right-minded' Allen should regard this wild wordy war with feelings of astonishment and indignation, was natural.— His emotions, all fresh and pure from the unadulterated fountains of nature, he listened to some of the leading orators of the day with wondering awe, mingled with contempt and wrath. On comparing the sentiments and patriotism of these windy, mindless, principleless declaimers with the men of the old republics, or with our own high-souled Revolutionary fathers, he saw few, or none, of those great and shining qualities of mind and heart that had commanded his own confidence and respect, and which he supposed ought to have had the same effect on other minds. The manner in which he expressed his opinion of the party action of his countrymen, in several letters to his friends, and essays for the press, gave a pleasing proof of his sterling integrity, sound judgment and manly patriotism. In conversation and correspondence with his friends, he frequently remarked that he could not appreciate the patriotism, or even discretion of those political gladiators, who from every stump, traduced the character and detracted from the great actions of some of our patriot-fathers, whose virtue, knowledge and services, have given them a renown as wide as the world and as long as time. Nor could he refrain from doubting the motives and faith of men who professed to admire, as great and superior, some of the most equivocal specimens of our race.

As a student of his country's history, his reading taught him to revere the character and be grateful for the services of some of the men, living and dead, whom he heard denounced, by partizan orators, for the basest conduct and most unpatriotic designs. In this category were names of those belonging to both parties, but much the largest number to one of them. He felt called on, under such circumstances, to review his opinions. He did so, and guided by the records of history, rather than the passion and ribaldry of party, the result of his inquiries attached him still more firmly to principles he had already adopted from an honest conviction of their truth. In a speech made in Lawrence county, near the residence of his father in the Spring of 1845, he gave utterance to his opinions on this subject, in nearly the following words:

"The pictured pages of Livy and other ancients, have held up for the admiration or execration of all future times, the good and bad men engaged in high official stations in those times. The great and good men whom they admired, were commended by their fellow-citizens, for acquirements and actions when then indicated, and will ever indicate their wisdom and worth. The same great qualities which prompted those ancient worthies in their usefulness, will command the admiration and repeet of all good men, so long as virtue and truth shall be esteemed. The sages and patriots of our own country, who practised the same virtues, displayed the same tal-

ents and performed similar actions among us, have received, and should continue to receive our sincerest grat-
gratitude and respect. What can it signify to men,
knowing and loving the truth, how party spite and hate
may revile the memory of our Jeffersons and Jacksons,
our Adams' and Clays. There stand the enduring monuments of their presence and performances; there; are
the pictures history, impartial history, has drawn of them.
In regard to some of them we yet have the traditions of
fathers, all concurring in commendation of those whom
mad ambition and party rancor now assail. Let us, my
friends, stand by the old paths. We know that our Revolutionary fathers were pure patriots. They would never
have recommended to the confidence of their offspring,
men and sentiments so base and false, as party men now
assert those were and are. No, no, no. Our patriot-
fathers knew who and what they esteemed was worthy,
and they have commended to us only truth and virtue,
and their ablest advocates. We should not, we will
never surrender the renowned names and shining actions
of our revolutionary patriots to the aimless eulogy, or to
the angry, groundless execrations of mere partizans. If
their contemporaries esteemed and trusted them, and
have transmitted their names to us as patriots, they were
worthy. If worthy then, not all the malevolent eloquence
of pandemonium should—shall it?—wring them from
our embraces.''

As a student of political economy, Mr. Allen knew that
the wisest and best patriots who formed the Constitution
of the Union, repeatedly refused to insert in that instrument a power for Congress to charter a Bank. He
knew, as all may know who will read history, that Mr.

Luther Martin, a delegate to the Convention of 1787, from the State of Maryland, and several other distinguished members complained to their constituents, and that some of them left the Convention *because* it refused to insert this power in the Constitution. He knew that the same arguments for and against paper money—especially when to be issued by the government—had been urged before the Convention; that paper money proved injurious to every country which had used it, and that it had been the cause of immense injury in our own country during the Revolution and since. He knew that Washington, Madison and Jefferson had discountenanced its manufacture by the Federal Government, and that these and other of the Revolutionary patriots, feared the advocates of paper money would persuade the people to reject the Constitution, *because it withheld from Congress the power to charter a Bank*, and that some of our sages have written arguments against giving such power to Congress, that never have been answered or attempted to be answered.* Resting his political faith upon these unquestioned and unquestionable authorities, Mr. Allen became an ardent and bold friend of the men who undertook to sustain the opinions and measures he approved. Few men of his age were listened to by the popular assemblies with more attention; none enjoyed a larger

---

* Opinion of Jefferson, Secret Debates, pp. 9, 57, 79, 220, 246 and 256. Madison Papers, III, pp. 129, 1344 to 1346, 1442, 1542 and 1615. Washington's Writings, IX, pp. 187, 231, 233 and 246. The venerable H. L. White, in his celebrated speech of 1832, cited these authorities, and adopted them as a just expression of his opinions. The subject was at that time fully discussed in Congress, by the press and on the stump, during the canvass of General Jackson for his second term, and the people clearly adopted the views of Jefferson.

E

share of their confidence. Treating the opinions and character of antagonists with courtesy and respect, he was never known to have drawn upon him their enmity; but while he combated their opinions, he maintained with them the most friendly relations.

CHAPTER V.

Capt. Allen is nominated for the Legislature—His position on the Oregon and Texas questions—His Election.

In the Spring of 1845, when scarcely eligible by his age for a seat in the General Assembly, he was nominated by the people of his County, and elected their Representative, over a competitor of long standing and superior advantages. The canvass was conducted with great activity on both sides. The subjects discussed took in the whole range of State and National questions, the domestic and foreign policy and relations of the country; but the occupation of Oregon and the annexation of Texas, were by far the most exciting, as they were the most important topics at that time.

The claim of the United States to Oregon, was, by the party to which Mr. Allen belonged, said to be clear and unquestionable, from the 42° of North latitude, to 54° 40′. This claim rested on the Spanish title, as the first discoverers and occupants, as well as upon the discovery of Captain Grey, an American mariner who ranged the coast, landing at several points in 1791. The Spanish claim to the first discovery of Oregon, goes back to the year 1542. Friar Nica, a few years before, reported to the Viceroy of New Spain, that he had visited a rich and populous country lying North of New Spain. A fleet under Alarcon, and a land party under Coronado, were sent by the Viceroy to conquer the country. Again in 1542, the same officer sent Cabrillo on a voyage of discovery along the West coast of California. He proceeded as far North as 42ᵒ. *

In 1588, Maldonado pretended to have sailed from the Atlantic to the Pacific, via Hudson's Strait and a Western passage in 75ᵒ North latitude. This voyage, as well as that of Juan de Fuca, who is said to have made the same passage, was long considered fabulous, but more recent explorations render them probable. Vancouver afterwards, (in 1791,) attached Juan's name to the Strait, which it still bears. In 1775, Heceta Bodega y Quadra, sent by the Viceroy of New Spain, explored the Western coast as far as 57ᵒ 58'.† The next visitor was Captain Grey, who took the sloop Washington, of Boston, into the Straits of Fuca, in 1788, and in the Columbia, in 1791, discovered the celebrated river to which he gave the name of his vessel. During the latter year, Malispina was sent to explore the Nort-western coast, and the next year other voyages were made for the same purpose, and to verify the statement of Maldonado. All these explorations were made by Spain, who had also some stations on the coast before any other nation. In 1789, McKenzie crossed the Rocky Mountains from Canada, and reached the Pacific in 56ᵒ North—beyond the limits of Oregon. In 1804–1806, Captains Lewis and

---

* It was not until 1578, that Sir Francis Drake ranged the same coast, from 38ᵒ to 43ᵒ.

† This point is nearly four degrees North of the North boundary of Oregon. It was not till 1776, that Cook made his voyage. He began his survey in Nootka Sound, and proceeded Northward. The Russians had made some voyages 1727 and 1741, under Behring. They also discovered the Allentian and Fox Islands, but probably visited no part of the present territory of Oregon. Hearne in 1770–1772, reached the mouth of the Coppermine river, in about 69ᵒ North latitude.

Clarke were sent by the then President, Mr. Jefferson to explore the country. They passed the Rocky Mountains at about the 46° degree, and descended the Columbia to its mouth. Not long afterwards, an establishment was founded at the mouth of the Columbia, by Mr. Astor, of New York, which was continued until captured by a British force during the last war with that power. The British retained possession until 1818, when they surrendered it back to us under the provisions of the treaty.

From this view, it is seen that if any one discovered Oregon, it was not England. Spain undoubtedly made the first explorations and the first settlements. The exploration of Lewis and Clarke, in conjunction with the voyage of Pike up the Arkansas and Red rivers, were designed by the sage of Monticello, to acquire a correct knowledge of the extensive tract then recently acquired by us, under the name of Louisiana. The historical reader and politician will remember that the opponents of Mr. Jefferson opposed this acquisition, and predicted all manner of evils to the Union in consequence of its enlargement. The reports of the expedition were ridiculed, and the facts stated disputed. The idea of a mass of iron, salt or copper, now so well known, existing in those distant regions, was made the subject of jest and caricature. The sentiments and opinions then diffused, in spite of their known fallacy, are still urged upon the people with as much pertinacity and as little truth or reason as at first.

During his canvass before the people for a seat in the Legislature, Mr. Allen affirmed, and his antagonist denied the claim of the United States to Oregon, as founded on the foregoing historical facts and references. In several of his speeches, he displayed an accurate and minute knowledge of this part of our history, that reflected great credit on him, and tended to enlighten the public mind, and disabused it from the fallacious and factious fabrications of careless and ill informed minds. It was assumed by the party to which he was opposed:

1. That we had no color or claim to Oregon, never having occupied, discovered or claimed it as part of our territory.

2. That if it were ours it was worthless, and too distant and inaccessible to warrant a contest with England for its possession.

3. That to take possession of Oregon would subject our commerce to be swept from the Ocean, and the whole of our maritime towns to be ravaged and burnt by the British fleets.

In reply to the first proposition, Mr. Allen, in common with his party, contended that our claim rested on a clear and sound title, either as derived from Spain, or in our own right. The right of Spain rested on her first discovery, exploration and occupation of the coast from California to Vancouver or Quadra Island, as far North as 58°, before any other nation had visited or claimed the country. This claim had passed to us by treaty.— In addition to this, Captain Grey, an American mariner, discovered the river Columbia, and if any part of this Continent remained still open for occupation—which he denied—we must hold it according to the acknowledged rules, long established and acted on by the first occupying nations.

The first of these rules is—That the discovery and settlement of the mouth of a river entering the Ocean, gives the discoverer a right to the lands on both banks of such river and its tributaries, from its mouth to its source.

The second rule is—That the right so acquired precludes any other nation from interfering with, or purchasing land from the Indians, located within said limits.

The third rule is—That where another nation shall have a settlement on the same coast where such a discovery and settlement is made, the middle point between their settlements, *on the coast*, shall be the dividing line.

These positions were assumed to be the settled rules of national law, by Mr. Adams in his discussions with Mr. Onis, the Spanish Minister, pending the Spanish treaty for the cession of Florida to us, and Texas to Spain. Onis admitted them, as did Mr. Clay in his speech on the treaty, in the Senate; and it is believed they have never been questioned by any nation since their incorporation into the law of nations. Tested by these rules, our title to Oregon is infinitely better than that of England to many of her vast colonial possessions.

In reply to the second assumption, that the possession of Oregon was not worth a contest, it might have been sufficient to ask, if we were to suffer even a worthless part of our territory to be wrested from us, what would our national character be worth? But time and events have placed numerous and cogent arguments in our power. The trade in peltries, carried on across the frozen regions of the Northern part of the Continent, has been the source of immense wealth to those so engaged. They have shipped their supplies from Europe via Canada, and sent them into the interior by means of canoes and on the backs of Indians, and received their returns in peltries, on the Atlantic, by the same mode of conveyance, subject to numerous delays and dangers of the sea, lakes, rivers and the savages along their route, and then transmitted their furs and peltries by sea to Europe, China or elsewhere for a market. This course of trade, besides the dangers, involved a vast waste of time and means. Yet it was profitable—more so than many other branches of commerce. Had the British companies who carried it on, been at liberty to avail themselves of a more Southern route, in a milder climate, and of our rivers for transportation, the dangers and delays would have been diminished and the profits augmented. These advantages are secured to our citizens, who, by the exclusion of foreigners, will enjoy the Indian trade in our own limits without competition.— During the joint use of ours and the British people, the best positions became the subject of controversy, ending in violence, often in outrages on persons and property of the most heinous character. All these evils are removed by our occupation, and our citizens can, as they are already beginning to do, proceed directly from the mouth of the Columbia to China, Australia and the East Indies with their peltries, and bring their return cargoes to the market without the necessity of transhipment, and in much shorter time and less risk of every kind. If the trade of this region was an object to those who conducted it under so many disadvantages, it surely must be more valuable to us who may pursue it under more favorable circumstances. Nor is this all. The heights of the Rocky Mountains will be passed by Rail-roads, opening a short and safe commercial way from the Atlantic cities to the ports of China and the East, whence the teas, spices and other goods of those countries may reach our markets in six or eight weeks instead of eight or twelve months. By this route the Eastern goods will reach us fresher, and will be cheaper than when coming by way of the old route, round the Cape of Good Hope or Cape Horn. These advantages must make a change in the course of trade to the Asiatic countries. Instead of sending to Europe for Eastern goods, our merchants will furnish the markets of Europe. The great desideratum which led to the discovery of America—the search for a more direct way to the East—will have been supplied. This way will pass from the Atlantic to the Pacific through the centre of our country. The routes via the Isthmus of Suez and the Red Sea will be abandoned. Instead of the ships of England and Bedouin camels, our steam cars and boats will become the carriers in this immense trade. The immense amount of timber, coal and iron abounding along the new line of travel, will appreciate in value, and vast quantities now wasted or unsaleable will become a source of wealth. The tall trees of Oregon, its cereals will accompany its peltries to the ports of China, and be there exchanged for teas, rich stuffs and specie. The iron, copper and lead of Missouri, with the coal of Ohio, Pennsylvania and Virginia, will swell the flood of commerce to which the new route will give new impetus, new means, new objects and immense increase.

To the third assumption, that a controversy with England would lead to the destruction of our commercial and maritime towns, it was sufficient to ask if our flag must be lowered merely to appease the growling of the British lion. National honor must be maintained at every hazzard.

With these and similar arguments, Mr. Allen met his antagonist before the people, who heard him everywhere with pleased attention. The annexation of Texas led to discussions as animated, perhaps more so, because the supposed danger was nearer, and for that reason greater. This was the leading question, while it was pending, throughout the Union. Its nature and magnitude, the immense interests and consequences involved in its decision, the alledged efforts of European powers to control the decision, all tended to increase the excitement which pervaded the popular mind.

In the discussion of the Annexation of Texas, the heart as well as the head of Mr. Allen was warmly enlisted. It was his enthusiasm on this question which hurried him, whilst a college student, to forget the rules of the institution and to enter the arena of public debate. It was a subject well calculated to fire the enthusiasm of a young man of ardent temperament. He was familiar with the outrages which had been perpetrated upon the early Texas settlers. He had sympathised deeply with them in their sufferings. He had watched with earnest solicitude their struggles with the Indians and Mexicans— their valor had won his warmest admiration, and their brilliant victory of San Jacinto had enshrined them in his heart as noble heroes and patriots. He had been taught by his father to admire the character of the gallant hero of that splendid victory. He cherished for the people of Texas the affection awarded to kindred.

With such feelings, Mr. Allen entered the canvass for the Legislature with the flag of "the lone star" streaming over his head. He had hailed the application of Texas for admission into the Union with joy, and all the energies of his enthusiastic soul were engaged in her cause. It need not be said that on such a theme he was eloquent— the theme itself was eloquent. A few brave adventurers had left their homes and their kindred in the United

States, and through scenes of blood and carnage they had conquered a Republic from the Indians and Mexicans. They now returned to their father-land and tendered an empire as the reward of their sufferings and valor. The question was, whether the tender should be accepted, or whether these noble sons of noble sires should be spurned and rejected? The generous hearts of the American people were open for their reception, but the voice of party policy was raised against it. This was the leading issue in the Presidential contest of 1844, and the result was the annexation of Texas to the United States. To justify this result was the business of Mr. Allen in his canvass for the Legislature.

In the investigation of this subject Mr. Allen brought to bear a depth of research, a power of reasoning and a force of eloquence which rendered his speeches irresistible. He showed that by the law of nations, Texas had won an indisputable title to her Independence—a title which even Mexico had not dared to contest for nine years—a title as incontrovertible as that on which rested the claim of the United States to national existence—a title which had been freely recognized by all the leading powers of the old world. He exposed the pretensions set up by Mexico to the sovereignty of Texas, and adduced strong reasons for believing that other governments were seeking to profit by defeating her annexation to the United States. He treated the threats of invasion made by Mexico with contempt, and insisted that if the question was divested of its party character in the United States, no Mexican army would ever have the temerity or the folly to invade the soil of Texas. He showed that the question as to whether the Rio Grande or the Neuces was the true boundary of Texas belonged alone to the politicians of the United States, whilst the government of Mexico set up a claim to the whole territory of Texas.— He insisted that if Mexico should be so rash or so foolish as to make war for the re-conquest of Texas, the people of the United States would be bound by every principle of justice and honor to resist and punish the invaders.— He entered fully and eloquently into the question of slavery as connected with the extension of our territory, maintaining that the adoption of the Missouri Compromise line in the resolutions of annexation ought to be acquiesced in as equitable by the whole country. His arguments on the general question of enlarging our territorial limits by new acquisitions were profound and unanswerable. He maintained that the fears entertained by some politicians from giving too great an extent to our territory were without foundation, and that under the federative feature in our Constitution, new States may be safely added until our republic shall reach from ocean to ocean, and the Union will remain as firm as ever.

These were the leading subjects of national moment discussed by Mr. Allen in his canvass, and these were some of the positions which he enforced. In regard to local subjects, his attention was directed [mainly to the rights and interests of the occupant settlers, many of whom resided in his county. On this subject he felt a deep concern, and it may be safely said, that the occupants never had a more sincere and ardent advocate.— He had been reared amongst them, he understood their character thoroughly, he knew their rights, and he fully comprehended the claims which they had on the government for protection. His own open, frank, generous and ardent nature was to the occupants the best guaranty that in his hands they would have a faithful friend.

There were circumstances connected with the contest between Mr. Allen and Mr. Buchanan, which gave to it unusual interest at home and abroad. Mr. Allen was barely eligible by his age to a seat in the Legislature.— His competitor was in the meridian of life, a gentleman of unimpeachable character, having been honored by the people of Lawrence again and again, and having filled with distinguished credit the office of Speaker of the House of Representatives. His reputation for talents was well established not only in his own county but throughout the State, and his popularity was such, that he was generally regarded as invincible. In this election the political complexion of the State was conceded on both sides to be doubtful, and the result in the county of Lawrence might turn the scale. Under such circumstances the selection of so young a man as Mr. Allen to contend against such fearful odds, shows how strongly he had secured the confidence of his political friends. He accepted the nomination with reluctance, because he doubted his ability to meet the crisis successfully, but having yielded to the earnest appeals of his friends, he entered upon the work with an energy and enthusiasm which gave strong assurances of success. It was one of the most animated, exciting and interesting contests that has ever taken place in the State. To the last moment it was doubtful on which side victory would fall, and when the votes were counted it was found that Mr. Allen had triumphed by six votes! The result was hailed throughout the State by his political friends as a most brilliant achievement. By the result he had established a character for indomitable energy and perseverance, for unspotted integrity, for high and commanding talents, and for enthusiastic devotion to democratic principles. His name was familiar to his political friends in every part of the State, and when the Legislature met he was astonished to find how deep an interest had been felt in his success.

CHAPTER VI.

Capt. Allen's course in the Legislature—His speech on the Occupant Question—Returns to his Law Books—Call for Volunteers—His speech on the War.

WHEN the General Assembly convened on the 1st Monday of October 1845, Mr. Allen took his seat as a member. He was the youngest Representative in the House,
and was elected under circumstances well calculated to
excite the vanity of one whose mind was not well bal-
anced. No such effect, however, was observable in the
conduct of Mr. Allen. His demeanor was modest, retiring and unassuming. He listened cheerfully to the
counsels of experience, and he profited by it. He fully
comprehended the importance to himself of a course
which should comport with his age, and hence he made
it a point to address the House but seldom, and when he
did speak, to be prepared. In his intercourse with members, he was easy and sociable; in his manners, open,
frank and sincere in his conversation; strictly virtuous in
his sentiments, and scrupulously moral in his associations
and habits. His speeches on every occasion evinced
mature reflection and profound thought. He was scrupulously regular in his attendance upon the sittings of
the House, and always watchful as to the progress of
business. Whilst he constantly increased his reputation
for talents, he secured the name of a business member.

It is impossible for the writer to allude to various interesting measures of legislation, in the discussion of

which Mr. Allen took a prominent part. But we cannot forego the pleasure of referring especially to his course on the question of protecting the rights of the Occupant settlers. On this subject he felt and manifested a deep solicitude, and his sentiments will be found fully expressed in the following able Speech, delivered by him in the House of Representatives :

REMARKS OF MR. ALLEN,

On an amendment offered by himself to a Memorial from the Senate, in regard to the Public Lands.

Mr. Speaker:—It seems to me that the prime object for which the memorial just read was intended, has been entirely overlooked. It merely asks the Congress of the United States for a relinquishment of the vacant and refuse lands to the State of Tennessee, for the specific purpose of endowing and building up a College in the Western District, at Jackson. I will not offer reasons why an amount of forty thousand dollars shall not be granted to that division of the State for the very laudable object proposed in the memorial. But I do earnestly insist on my amendment, asking for a prolongation of time allowed to occupant holders to make payment for their claims. It would be a mere reiteration of sentiment expressed by me on a former occasion, to say that I am in favor of the passage of a memorial that has for its object an extension of the time allowed to settlers to pay for their occupants at the price fixed by an act of Congress, under which Tennessee is constituted the agent of the Government of the United States, to issue grants and perfect titles to the same. The resolutions which I had the honor of introducing, raising a select committee, with instructions to report favorably in behalf of occupancy, evince the feeling by which I am actuated in securing to those upon public land the peaceful and undisturbed possession of their homes. But for this incentive, I should not have presumed to tax the patience of the House with a single remark. A consciousness of imperative duty to those whose wishes I have the honor of representing upon this floor, demands that I should not be silent under such circumstances as those by which I am encompassed. To let the subject pass without an expression of my humble convictions, I would feel as if I were faithless and insincere towards an enlightened constituency. This is no new question. It has hitherto excited the faithful and studious attention of the purest and best men of the land, and it calls upon *us*, in language not equivocal, to give further indulgence to settlers to pay for their occupants. I do not believe, and never can, without contradictory testimony, that Representatives upon this floor are disposed to resist a call that strikes, with such force upon their minds, and agitates every noble feeling that belongs to our nature.

The exigency of the occasion—the unenviable condition of our people resting upon the precarious tenures by which their homes are held—and the inevitable force of circumstances too powerful to be disregarded, demand that the Legislature should, as far as it can, interpose its arm to protect them from the unjust encroachments of the speculator. These things speak a language that commands merited respect—a language that appeals to us cogently and persuasively. They ask, they implore us, sir, who are the legitimate guardians of their interests, not to reject the petitions that are emanating from every cottage in the western and a portion of the middle division of our noble and chivalrous State—petitions,

F

upon an inconsiderate rejection of which, many warm hearts will be made to bleed, and many industrious and virtuous families bereft of the "sweets of a home."—Coming, as I do, fresh from the society of those about whom I have been speaking, I cannot be insensible of the embarrassing circumstances that attend them. They are, it is true, poor, but strictly and rigidly honest.—They participate alike with you, sir, and every disinterested patriot in this broad land, in whatever conduces to exalt and dignify the American character. They abjure, in truth and in fact, oppression under any of its Protean forms and disguises. At all times and under every emergency, they hold themselves in readiness to defend their honored and beloved country from the unprovoked and ruthless attacks of an insulting foe. Many of them have already given indication of their inherent devotion to their country on the memorable plains of New Orleans and other sanguinary conflicts in that war, which reflected a radiancy of glory around that proud State in whose emporium we are now convened. But why speak of these things? Are they not fresh and vivid in the recollection of every member entitled to a seat upon this floor?

Mr. Speaker, they claim nothing for what they have done or suffered. Patriotism is ever disinterested, and asks no remuneration for its sacrifices. Its fires will ever burn upon the altar of brave hearts when liberty itself is no more. Considerations of this character may pass for what they are worth. I have repeated, that the mass of the people South and West of the Congressional Reservation Line, are poor. In confirmation of this asservation, I need only appeal to those whose opportunities have been sufficient to ascertain their true condition.—

They all unite with me in expressing the conviction that they will not be able to save their occupants by the first of next July.

In such an emergency, the question naturally arises, what is to be done? What *can* be effected most congenial to the wishes of the people, and compatible with the interest of the country? Shall we, *can* we say, that because they have had sufficent time and failed, they shall have no further indulgence? Our government will be influenced by no such paltry considerations. She will *ever* throw the broad, impenetrable ægis of protection around her own patriotic citizens. Under existing circumstances, what policy is it best for us to adopt? The pioneer settler is not to be neglected. Shall the only ray of comfort that dawns upon him from a cloudless sun be obscured by Legislative indifference? The question is not difficult of solution. No man can brook the thought of thousands of our fellow-citizens being unceremoniously dispossessed of their homes—of being snatched away, ruthlessly and mercilessly, from those sacred and fascinating retreats around which memory lingers with delight. It is too revolting to the feelings—too painful for endurance. We hope for better things. We anxiously look forward to brighter and more halcyon days. The unobtrusive cottage upon some bleak hill or solitary waste, be it ever so humble, is a palace to the poor man. It belongs to *him*—to *him* and his children after him.— That by granting further extension of time they will be better able to indemnify their claims, we cherish the most gratifying and reasonable hope. Unless indulgence is afforded, it is useless to disguise the fact that the condition of the occupant claimant will be deplorable. This is no stretch of the imagination. It is truth unvarnished and unadorned.

The better and larger portion of our public domain has already been occupied at the government price, and the "rest and residue" is generally of a refuse character. It may be years to come before it would be settled under the provision of the present undefined law. Every consideration of policy and expediency require a further reduction in the price. It will greatly advance the interest of the State in various ways, which I will not *now* stop to consider. Upon the broad grounds of expediency, we base the success of this question.

When our country is invaded by an insulting foe— when our soil is desecrated by the approach of a tyrant who boastingly threatens destruction and carnage—when the green graves of our immortal ancestry, who fought the battles of freedom, whose blood stained the field of valor and won for them undying glory, are to be disturbed—dishonored—whose sword is it that leaps instantaneously from its scabbard to repel the invader?—whose arm is not nerved for the conflict, and whose bosom is not ready to breast the fury of the storm? The humble and obscure citizen, unknown to fortune and to fame, in whom patriotism is a virtue, and cowardice a crime, tenders his services at the first call, and forsakes family and friends to rescue his country from impending danger, or nobly perish in the trial.

This is the man around whom we desire the government to throw the panoply of its protection. There is no violation of faith, nor constitution—no tarnishing of national escutcheons—no obliteration of the stars and stripes that form a constellation upon our eagle-banner, connected with the successful termination of this transcendently important question. I have viewed it in all its dimensions and proportions, and am ready to sustain it.

I know that the fearful destiny of thousands hang suspended upon our deliberation upon this subject. Let us pass this memorial, with the amendment, and in time to come the people will bless our memories for it. As for myself, I can return home to the bosom of a proud and free constituency, and tell them upon this question I was not ignorant of my duty, and knowing I discharged it faithfully and fearlessly."

Upon the adjournment of the Legislature, early in 1846, Mr. Allen returned to his home in Lawrence county. He was greeted by his constituents with a cordial welcome, and a hearty approval of the manner in which he had discharged the trust committed by them to his hands. He had faithfully redeemed every pledge he had made to them, and had shown that their confidence in him was not misplaced. Many who had been politically opposed to him, were foremost in awarding to him their warm approval of the industry, ability and fidelity with which he had served them and watched over their interests. That which a patriotic public servant most highly prizes—the voluntary and hearty approbation of his constituents—it was the fortune of Mr. Allen to enjoy. He had the high gratification of knowing that his labors were appreciated, and that he had added greatly to his prosperity.

It had been the purpose of Mr. Allen when he closed his collegiate course, to qualify himself for the legal profession. In consenting to become a candidate for the Legislature, he did not abandon the profession. When his labors as a Legislator terminated, he turned his attention with promptness and avidity to his law books, looking forward with anxiety to the time when he could enter upon the profession to which he had dedicated his life. The study of the law is usually regarded as dry and uninteresting, but to Mr. Allen it was not so. He found nothing forbidding in the abstruse pages of Blackstone. Whilst he was charmed with the beauty and purity of his style, he found in his volumes, the development of a science which rested upon the labors of many of the most exalted intellects that ever lived. He did not take up his law book as he would a novel—to go through the mechanical process of running his eyes over the pages, and gathering at a glance the thread of the story, and in a hand-gallop tracing it to its final *denouement*. He took up his book as a student, remembering that what he was about to read had cost the master-spirits of the profession years of intellectual toil, and knowing that the beauties of the science could only be appreciated by a thorough comprehension of the eternal principles of right and justice, which lay at the foundation of the system. The study of the Law is irksome only to those who are averse to mental labors; but Mr. Allen derived his highest pleasure from that intense application of the mind which develops hidden truths, and hence he neither yawned over Blackstone nor dreamed over Chitty, but read and studied them with delight. He engaged in the study of the Law with a proper appreciation of the dignity of the profession, and with a firm determination to honor his calling.

It was whilst Mr Allen was assiduously engaged in preparing for the practice of the Law that he received intelligence of the invasion of our soil by the Mexican army, in crossing the Rio Grande. He did not stop to calculate the chances, or to consider the hardships or dangers of war, but made up his mind with promptness, to respond to any call which the Government might make for volunteer troops. His feelings upon receiving the intelligence, may be best gathered from the following extract of a speech which he prepared, and which he left amongst his papers. After describing the consummation of the Annexation of Texas under the figure of a marriage ceremony, he proceeds as follows:—

Now that the nuptial rites are celebrated and the conviviality of which it was the occasion, what now do we hear? Gross murmurs of irreconcileable hostility on the part of Mexico, who has been unfriendly to the United States, and an implacible enemy of Texas. Those who have been lawfully joined together in holy wedlock, she presumes to put assunder. Gents, an armed soldiery of Mexicans have planted their standard upon American soil. The American army under the command of Gen. Taylor is beleaguered. The war cry has been raised— intense excitement prevails, no doubt all over the Union. Our citizens are marching towards the invading army resolving to carry the war into the enemy's territory, and plant the star-spangled banner upon the walls of the Montezumas. Thousands of brave hearts are now heating with anxiety for the call upon their valor and patriotism—and when the proclamation does go forth, from one end of the Union to the other, brave hearts and strong arms will be ready to obey the summons. Men will rise up like the embattled hosts of Rhoderic Dhu, with the patriotic determination to unsheathe the sword, and in obedience to the command of the Grecian matron to her son, to return with them, or to return upon them. Whether they approved of the marriage or not, they are unwilling to see Texas exposed to spoliation, insult and injury.—

Rather than this, they would be for waging a worse than Trojan war. Split up, as we have been by party, our enemies, no doubt, vainly imagined that we were a divided people. But thanks to the indomitable patriotism of our people, when war's dread clarion is sounded, there is but one voice and one heart in this country, and that is an American voice and an American heart. There is but one banner under which they rally, and that is the banner of the country which waved in triumph in the dark hour of the revolution.

> Forever float that standard sheet!
> Where breathes the foe but falls before us,
> With Freedom's soil beneath our feet,
> And Freedom's banner streaming o'er us!

It was a remark of Lord Nelson at the battle of Trafalga, that England expects every man to do his duty. Let that be the motto to actuate us: that the United States expects every man to do his duty, and if he will do that, victory will be inscribed in golden characters upon our unfurled banner.

From the manifestation of enthusiastic ardor and the ebulition of patriotic feeling, I cannot cherish the semblance of a doubt, but the call will meet with a prompt response. What, Gents, is your determination? Who is willing to go—who? The same spirit which actuated the brave and dauntless Indian chief Conanchet, will actuate you, "we will fight," says he, "to the last man, rather than become servants to the English." The patriotic sentiment of Old Armstrong who fell wounded at the battle of Enotochipco, will awake similar emotions in your bosoms:—"Boys," says he, "some of you may fall, but save the cannon. Some of you may fall in the struggle, but let it be like brave men, with your face to

the enemy." I have no fears of the engagement.—
Should it be our pleasure to participate in the glories of
that war, we need but write back to our friends and relations at home, that we came, and like the Roman general, we saw and conquered. Do you want lessons of
fortitude and self-sacrificing devotion to country? Do
you ask for examples of magnanimous and lofty bearing?
If you do, I would point you to the gallant Lawrence,
who wrapped himself up in his country's flag and exclaimed, "don't give up the ship." I would point you
to Wertherford an Indian chief in the late war, &c.

What a commentary is this upon Tennessee chivalry?
A few more words, Gents, and I have done. I have
occupied, by the authority of the people, a station—a responsible station in the councils of the State of Tennessee. For this mark of their confidence, I hope I ever
shall be, and am truly thankful. I never shall forget it,
let me be placed under whatever circumstances I may.
When I forget it, may my right arm forget its coming,
and my tongue cleave to the roof of my mouth. May I
as soon forget the object that clings the nearest my affections. I can now say without regret and affectation,
that I cherish no political aspirations at all. I have no
personal advantage to seek—I desire none. All that I
now seek is, that I may be permitted to blend my destiny
with yours, whatever it may be. I surrender up any
personal comfort which I may enjoy, without a murmur
or complaint—"sink or swim, live or die, survive or perish," I have resolved and re-resolved to be among the
first to enlist my services in the defence of my injured
country. The decree has gone forth, and its mandates
will be obeyed.

CHAPTER VII.

Capt. Allen enlists as a Volunteer—Acted as Aid de Camp to
Gov. Brown—Declines the appointment of Quarter Master—
His Charge and Death at Monterey—Tributes to his Memory.

THE anticipated call for volunteer troops was soon
made, and Mr. Allen enlisted as a private soldier in the
Lawrenceburg Blues. This company was organized and
in readiness when the proclamation for Volunteers was
received. Its services were immediately tendered by
Capt. Alexander, and accepted by Gov. A. V. Brown.
At the appointed time, Capt. Alexander marched his gallant band of volunteers to the point of rendezvous, near
Nashville, where they were mustered into the service of
the United States. Upon the arrival of the various companies at Nashville, Gov. Brown appointed Mr. Allen his
special Aid de Camp during the stay of the troops at
their rendezvous near the city. He discharged the duties of the appointment until his company were embarked
for New Orleans, when he again resumed his position as
a private. He served in this capacity until the company
to which he was attached arrived at the encampment at
Lometa, Mexico, when Captain Alexander resigned his
command, and Mr. Allen was unanimously chosen as his
successor. He was not a candidate, nor did he desire the
command, but his companions in arms determined that
they would be led by him, and he yielded to their wishes.
Under the circumstances, this was the highest compliment which he could have received, and he so esteemed

it. He saw in it the high confidence which his comrades reposed in him, as well as their warm personal attachment to him. He determined that nothing but death should separate him from his command, and under this feeling of devotion to his companions, when President Polk tendered to him the rank of Major in the army, he declined the promotion. Writing to his father from Camargo, on this subject, he said: "I was gratified to learn that the President had given me the appointment alluded to in your letter. The rank and pay of Major ought to be considered as very desirable to some, but I cannot abandon my company for the highest appointment in the gift of the President. The boys say they will go under nobody else." All of his letters on his march, are characterized by the same lofty patriotism which breathes throughout the speech which has been quoted, whilst his allusions to his company are always in terms of the warmest affection. When about to leave Camargo for Monterey, he was compelled to leave behind about twenty of his company on account of sickness and debility. This was extremely painful to him, and in a letter to his father, he speaks thus feelingly of his comrades: " I have thirty-five or forty of my original company, who are still able to march with me. They feel like brothers to me. I regret to leave behind those who are on beds of affliction. I hope they will soon rejoin their friends. May the great God protect them and support them in all their trials and afflictions." Amongst the number thus left behind, was his brother, Sam Houston, to whom he was much devoted, and for whose safety he felt the deepest concern. In another letter from Camargo, about the same date, he refers to the fact that Gen. Pillow was left behind, in terms so complimentary to that brave officer, that it is due to him that the testimony should be record-ed. He says: "We will leave to-morrow or next day; we are placed under the command of Gen. Quitman, of Mississippi. Gen. Pillow is left behind. We all regret his being left behind. We want to be led by him and no other. He is the very man for the occasion. Although men have endeavored to prejudice the minds of the sol-diers against him previous to his arrival, he has proved be he very man for them. No man could be more pop-ular."

Accompanying this letter, Capt. Allen forwarded the following to the *Nashville Union:*

CAMP NEAR CAMARGO, Sept. 1, 1846.
To Brigadier Gen. G. J. PILLOW,

SIR:—Having been detached upon temporary duty, under the command of Brigadier Gen. Quitman, we deem it due no less to yourself than to the men under your command, to express to you our high sense of the value of your services, the sense of regret with which the officers of the first regiment of your Brigade, and the men under our command pass temporarily from under your command.

We assure you, sir, that we fully appreciate the un-ceasing exertions which you have made since assuming command of this Brigade, to relieve the distresses and afflictions of the sick, and your efforts to introduce and carry into effect, a proper system of discipline, and to fit your command for the active duties of the field. While we bear this testimony of our high regard for you per-sonally, and of the eminent qualifications for your com-mand, we assure you, that the men under our command concur with us in this expression of our views and feelings, and that there is not to our knowledge any diversity of opinion from these views in our regiment. We entertain the hope that you will be ordered forward with your Brigade in a short time, and that we will be restored to our proper place in your command, and if it be our fortune to participate in the conflicts with the enemy, that we may be led into the field of battle by Tennessee's own son, whose reputation, feelings and sympathies are identical with ours.

We remain most respectfully, yours, &c.

[Signed by all the Officers of the Regiment except one Company.]

The last letter written by Capt. Allen will be read with peculiar interest. It was addressed to his parents, and is as follows:—

SERALVO, MEXICO, Sept. 14th 1846.

MY DEAR PARENTS: I never wanted to see you so badly in my life. I arrived here yesterday with my company, together with the 1st Regiment Tennessee Volunteers. We leave here in the morning for Monterey. We are about 60 or 70 miles from Monterey, and about the same distance from Camargo. The battle will be fought in a few days. They (the enemy) are fortifying the place. They are reported as being ten or twelve thousand strong. Give my love to all my friends.

I have this day sent my resignation to the President, who appointed me Quarter-master. The boys are unwilling to be commanded by anybody else. By the grace of God, I will try and lead them without dishonor to victory.

I have a sword that was worn by my father, which shall not be dishonored in my hands.

Your son, WM. B. ALLEN

When this letter was written, it was well understood that a battle was to be fought in a few days. The tone which pervaded it shows the spirit in which Capt. Allen led his gallant company, one week after, in the bloody charge at Monterey. On the 21st of September, 1846, that charge was made, and whilst it resulted in one of the most brilliant victories which crowned the American arms in the Mexican war, it sent many brave spirits to a premature grave. Soon after the battle an officer, of the Lawrenceburg Blues addressed a letter to the father of Capt. Allen, which describes with so much minuteness the part borne by him in the charge, and the manner of his fall, that its insertion in full length becomes proper:

CAMP NEAR MONTEREY, MEXICO, ⎱
　　　　　　Oct. 5th, 1846. ⎰

DEAR SIR:—I embrace the present opportunity of writing you that you may know the state of the Lawrenceburg Blues at present. Our Captain, WM. B. ALLEN, with nine of the company, are numbered with the dead. Our encampment is situated between 3 and 4 miles from the forts and batteries of the city. On the 20th there was some reconnoitering and cannonading between the two armies, which lasted for two hours, when we retired to the camp with no loss. The eventful and long to be remembered morning of the 21st of September arrived. The volunteers were eager for the contest. We arrived in front of the forts and batteries—the Ohioans and Kentuckians on the right, the Tennesseans and Mississippians in the centre, the Baltimoreans and Regulars on the left. In that position we stood the cannonading for at least half an hour. There our brave and lamented Captain partook of a hearty meal said, "Boys if I die to-day I shall die with a full stomach." At that moment the Baltimoreans and Regulars were ordered to charge the batteries on the left, but shrunk back in confusion and dismay. The order Tennesseans had, left flank, left face, *charge men, charge.* Our company in front, and ever anon could our Captain's voice be heard saying, "*Come on my brave boys, come on, close up, close up.* In that position for near two miles, were we exposed to the raking fires of two batteries and the noted *black fort*, one ball taking effect in our company, which sent seven brave souls to eternity. Then again was the shout from our brave Captain heard through the smoke, "come on my brave boys, come on." About seventy yards from the fort the command halt was given, and then the fight with musketry commenced. Allen's voice was then again steadily heard saying, "Boys take good aim, don't let them fire that cannon again." And well they obeyed that command, for that cannon ceased to fire.— Our Captain was shot through the breast with a musket ball, and looking around said, "Boys, I must die," (and in another letter he said, "I am dying, hurra my brave boys.") He died bravely, with his sword unsheathed and firmly grasped in his hand. The word charge was then given, and Lawrence county has the honor of having the first man there. GEO. H. NIXON was the first man on the ramparts of that fort. There he flourished his sword and said, "boys come on, my brave boys, come on." I have only written as far as your son was concerned in the first day's battle. The letters and private property of Capt. Allen are now in the possession of Lt. Nixon, which will be taken care of and returned to you. Before his death I heard him often remark, that he had assured his father that that sword should never be dishonored in his son's hands; and that pledge has been fulfilled. The sword will again be returned to you, as it has been secured for that purpose. The following are the names of those killed and wounded belonging to the Lawrenceburg Blues: Killed—Capt. Wm. B. Allen, Finley Glover, Wm. Rhodes, J. B. Burkitt, J. M. L. Campbell, J. W. Wilson, A. J. Gibson, J. W. Saunders, A. J. Eaton, A. A. Pratt. Wounded--G. H. Nixon, slightly in the knee; M. D. Watson, in the thigh; J. M. Bailey, do; Jesse Brashears, in the head, (glanced) arm and back; J. W. Curtis, in the shoulder and foot; H. H. Dotson, shoulder; T. C. Ramsey, right arm shivered and amputated above the elbow; A. C. Richardson, do.; W. M. Alford, through the right side; M. C. Abernathy, thigh, slightly; A. S. Alexander, through the left arm; J. H. Kay, leg taken off above the knee; C. Boyd, thigh; J. Gavin, do.; Aaron Parks, shoulder, slightly; J. Vining, body and foot; F. Richardson, through thigh, badly; B. L. Cannon, slightly. They are all getting on finely and will no doubt get well.

D. HUBBARD,
O. S. Lawrenceburg Blues.

Such was the premature termination of the career of one of the most promising young men of the State.—Until his fall was announced, it was not known by his warmest friends how enviable a reputation he had formed. It is no exageration to say that the news of his death spread a general gloom over the State. By his election to the Legislature under the circumstances already detailed, by the commanding position which he occupied in that body, and by his prompt response to the call for volunteers, he had enlisted the warm interests of a wide

circle of friends throughout the State.   When the intelligence arrived, that young Allen had fallen, though he
had fallen gloriously, in the battle of Monterey, it filled
the hearts of thousands with grief.   A high destiny had
been predicted for him, and he was expected to return
home crowned with laurels—but how inscrutable are
the ways of Providence?   For some wise purpose, beyond motal ken, it was meet that the fond hopes of admiring friends and affectionate relations should be disappointed.   To such an afflicting dispensation, it becomes
all to bow with humility, and to derive from the manner
of his death, all the consolation that is afforded in knowing that he fell gloriously.   There was a sublimity in his
fall which no language can portray.   Many a hero has
been deified for exploits far less chivalrous than was
young Allen's daring charge.   He fell when the victory
was won, and his last words were worthy of a dying
hero.   When the fatal ball entered his breast, he fell firmly grasping the sword which had been worn by his venerable father, and with his last breath uttered a shout of
encouragement and victory, "Hurrah, my brave boys."

There is something touchingly melancholy in the death
of a young man of promise.   It blasts so many fond
hopes of parents and friends.   It makes an aching void
in the hearts of so many confiding associates—it disap-
points the expectations of so many admiring acquaintances.   But how much more painful is the shock, when
such an one falls suddenly, in the vigor of health, in a
foreign land, in the very act of achieving an exploit of
heroism which would have won for him influence and
honor through life.   It was the fate of young Allen so to
fall, and to terminate his short, but bright career.

G

The death of Capt. Allen called forth many warm tributes of respect for his memory, and many eloquent eulo-
giums upon his charcter, both in prose and verse. A
few of these may be appropriately inserted to show how
deeply his death was regretted, and how sincerely his virtues were admired.

The members of the Erosophian Society, attached to
the Nashville University, adopted the following tribute:

 EROSOPHIAN HALL, Nov. 21, 1846.

At the last regular meeting of the Society, the follow-
ing preamble and resolutions were introduced by Mr.
Robert Eakin Deery, in regard to the Death of Captain
WILLIAM B. ALLEN, and adopted:

WHEREAS—We have received the melancholy news of
the death of WILLIAM B. ALLEN, late a Captain in the
United States Army of Invasion, and who was for a number of years, a true, faithful and efficient member of this
Society; possessed of a fine order of talents and an indomitable energy combined with all the virtues that dignify man. And *whereas*, the sad tidings has thrown a
cloud of gloom and despondency over us, and reminded
us that the winged messenger Death, has plucked from
our midst one of our former associates, who was kind,
magnanimous and brave, and snatched from the State one
whose prospects for future usefulness and greatness were
bright and glowing. And *whereas*, his whole course in
College auguered a high destiny for him, and this was
in some degree strengthened by the fact that in a few
months after his graduation, he was chosen by the people who had long known him, and could appreciate his
worth, to represent them in the representative branch of
the last Legislature. Nor was his patriotism bounded by

a narrow circle. For when a call for Volunteers was made, he early enrolled himself, and met his death at Monterey while urging his men to victory. Although the sting inflicted, is soothed and chastened by the happy reflection that he fell gloriously fighting in his country's cause, yet we deeply and sensibly feel that his vacancy can never be filled, and in common with all his acquaintances, we not only mourn his loss to our Society, but to the State in general. Therefore,

Be it Resolved, That we tender to his bereaved parents our sincerest sympathies in the loss of so kind, affectionate and promising a son.

Be it Resolved, That as a token of our high esteem for his memory, we wear the usual badge of mourning for thirty days, and that the *"Star"* in the Hall be shrouded in mourning for the same length of time.

Be it Resolved, That a copy of these proceedings be forwarded to his parents, and also furnished the city papers for publication.

BENJ. F. PRICE, *Pres.*

C. L. DAUGHERTY, *Sec.*

Gov. Campbell, the Colonel-Commandant of the Regiment to which Capt. Allen had belonged, in a letter to his father, spoke as follows:—

CAMP ALLEN, NEAR MONTEREY,
October 26, 1846.

GEN. ALLEN—*Dear Sir:* You will long before this reaches you, have received the painful intelligence of the death of your worthy and gallant son, Capt. WILLIAM B. ALLEN, who fell in the attack upon Monterey, on the 21st of September last. He had, during his service in the army, distinguished himself by his kind and gentlemanly demeanor, and by his prompt and officer-like conduct; and when the day of battle came, he was at the head of his column, and lead it most gallantly to the charge made upon one of the enemies strong fortifications by the 1st. Regiment of Tennessee Volunteers, until the fatal shot from the enemy struck him down and deprived him of life. I deeply regret the death of that eminent and gallant officer, and sympathize most sincerely with you and his friends for his loss. He was a young man of great promise, and would, had he survived this campaign, have taken a very high rank in the estimation of his countrymen.

In a letter written from Camp Allen, in Mexico, Col. Anderson, the Lieutenant-Colonel of the Regiment, alluded to Capt. Allen as follows:

I had intended to say in my statement of the fight of the 21st, that when within some four hundred yards of the fort, a cannon ball struck Capt. Allen's company, and cut down seven men, four of them were killed on the ground, and within some 130 yards of the fort, Captain Allen himself received a mortal shot and fell at the head of his company, leading it, as he was most gallantly, to the charge. In honor of his heroic bravery on that day, *our present encampment* has been named "Camp Allen." He deserves, as does all the brave sons of Tennessee, who fell on that day, an imperishable remembrance in the memory of every true patriot.

In an eloquent speech delivered by Col. Guild, of Sumner County, upon a proposition to erect a suitable Monument to commemorate the brave deeds of the volunteers from Sumner County, who had fallen in battle, he made the following beautiful allusion to Capt. Allen:

Among others who fell in that great charge, was Capt.
WM. B. ALLEN, of Lawrence. I served with him in our
last Assembly; I know him well, and no man who ever
did, but was his friend. His mind was richly stored
with all the learning of the day, united to a large and patriotic heart. He was not only the soul of honor, but
pink of chivalry. If he had survived that great battle,
there was no man of higher promise of future usefulness
to our State, or who would have shown forth a more brilliant star. Not only these but many other promising
young Tennesseans, now sleep in death. Although they
will never return, to light up and make cheerful the
houses of their parents, and enjoy the plaudits of their
country, yet they have left names, which are priceless
gems to their respective families, not only reflecting
honor upon them, but upon their country.

> " Ah how hard it is to climb,
> The steeps where fame's proud Temple shines afar,
> Ah, who can tell how many a heart sublime?
> Hath felt the influence of malignant star,
> And with fortune, waged an eternal war."

We saw our brave Tennesseans climb those heights,
we saw them arrive at the Temple, and with their lives
snatch the fame their patrotism sought. While we glory
in the honor they have acquired, and partake of the fame
they have given their country, we must deeply lament
their early death. It remains for a grateful country to
cherish their memories, and perpetuate their virtues.
We do so by erecting a suitable monument to our fallen
brave ; by so doing we not only indicate a proper feeling
of gratitude to those who have given their lives to their
country, but we show a proper appreciation of the noble
virtues which mark the patriot; it will excite the rising

generations to rally around the Eagle of their country,—
sustain our free institutions, and emulate the virtues of
these we intend to honor. These result swil lnot only
be produced, but by the erection of this monument we perpetuate the military fame of our State, which is blended
with our honored slain.

The editor of the *Columbia Beacon* announced the death
of Captain Allen in the following highly complimentary
terms:—

DEATH OF CAPTAIN ALLEN.

The death of this gallant young man who fell as he
was leading on his brave men to victory, has caused universal regret in our community, and throughout this
part of the State. He was one of Tennessee's noblest
sons. Although he had only arrived at the age of
twenty-three years, lacking a few months, he had made
for himself great character. He was one of the most
prominent members of the last Legislature, and was a
general favorite with his own party, and at the same time
he commanded the respect and esteem of his opponents.
His death has been lamented by his political opponents
as well as his political friends. So much was he attached to his men, and so much were they attached to him,
that although he was offered higher offices than the one
which he held, yet rather than leave his company, he declined the promotion. Such instances of devoted attachment as this are rarely met with. We have never known
the death of a young man to cause so deep a feeling of
sorrow, and be a source of such general grief. He had
received a liberal education, and gave every promise of
extensive usefulness and great distinction. But to those
who knew him best, with whom he mingled in the scenes

of private life, and who saw him around the domestic hearth, has his loss caused the greatest anguish. Twas not as a legislator nor as a soldier they saw in him his brightest qualities, but as an associate, and friend and relation. His parents have the consolation of knowing that he died fighting the battles of his country at the head of his brave company.

He was a member of the Cumberland Presbyterian Church, and had lived a life consistent with his high profession.

The writer of this portion of the sketch of the life of CAPT. ALLEN, was editior of the *Nashville Union* when the news of his death was received. He will be pardoned for inserting the poor, but heartfelt tribute, which he then paid to the memory of one to whom he had been warmly attached:—

From the Nashville Union.

CAPT. WILLIAM B. ALLEN.

It is difficult for us to realize the sad fact that this noble youth lies cold in the arms of death at Monterey—and the distressing truth cannot be resisted. WM. B. ALLEN has fallen, and sleeps the sleeep of death in a foreign land. He fell gloriously, whilst leading his brave company to victory, and if anything could blunt the keen anguish which his untimely death will produce in the bosoms of his venerable parents and his numerous relatives and friends, it will be the fact that he fell like a true solder, with his face to the enemy. We deplore his death as a sad calamity to the State—we had few such young men amongst us. He had scarce reached his twenty-first year, when he was honored by a seat in our last Legislature. In that body he distinguished himself by his assiduous devotion to the interests of his constituents, and by those unwavering evidences of high talents which he displayed in all the discussions in which he engaged. He had received a liberal education at the Nashville University, and his pathway to fame was rendered brighter and brighter to the hour of his death. When the call for Volunteers was made, he was prompt in enrolling himself for the battle-field. He became a favorite with all his comrades in arms. After becoming fully acquainted with his merits, he was chosen to lead the gallant company in which he volunteered as a private. He led that noble company into the city of Monterey, and there fell crowned with glory. The same energy and force of character which marked him out for some high destiny whilst he was yet a school-boy, signalized his whole course after he arrived to the age of maturity.— When he fell, gloriously leading our victorious troops, he had scarcely reached his twenty-third year—how bright were his propects? He had talents of the very first order—his mind was highly cultivated—he was calm, deliberate, prudent, yet energetic, industrious and ambitious of an honest fame. He was on the highway to the temple at whose shrine his generous and noble soul worshipped, and few at his age, have made so much progress in climbing the steep hill on whose top stands the temple. But in the midst of his brilliant career, in the very morning of his life, and whilst winning fresh laurels for his own brow in one of the hardest fought battles on record, he has been cut off—his bones are now resting with his brave comrades who fell by his side at Monterey, but his name will live as long as the world shall preserve its admiration of deeds of noble daring in the field of battle. We sympathise most sincerely with his afflicted parents—they have lost a son on whom they might well doat—he was their pride, and well he might be.— We lament his untimely death most sincerely—his loss is a calamity to the State. *He was our friend—tried and approved—true and faithful under all circumstances*—we shall never cease to cherish for his memory the warmest feelings of affection.

CHAPTER VIII.

Tributes of Respect to his Memory—Letter, &c., of M. C. Galloway, Esq.,—Ceremonies of his Funeral—Col. Rose's Address—His Brother, Sam Houston Allen's death.

IN the following poetical tributes, the reader will find how deeply imbedded Capt. Allen was in the hearts of his friends:

From the Columbia Observer.

DEATH OF ALLEN.*

BY DAVID R. ARNELL.

Before Monterey's walls he lay,
    Between the dark and light,
And the smile that lit the Soldier's brow
    Illumin'd the Land of Night;—
For he saw in his sleep the squadrons sweep
    Through the rush of the morrow's fight.

He snatched from its sheath his bright blue blade,
    When the drum first tapped Reveil,
And he saw the city a league away,
    In the dawn-light dim and pale,
And the flags borne on by the marsh'ling hosts,
    Like clouds in a driving gale.

He saw them marching slowly down
    The hill, and his soul could feel

---

* Capt. WILLIAM B. ALLEN, of Lawrence County, who was killed in the late brilliant action at Monterey. We hope our respect and friendship for the brave young officer, will be considered a sufficient apology for the appearance of the above Poem, though, to say sooth, we could have wished the tribute had fallen from an abler pen.   D. R. A.

A thrill of awe at those moving forms,
  And those ranks of bristling steel,—
"Oh, fear of death! should a man," he said,
  "With girlish faintness reel?"

And then in a martial tone, he spake,
  "Brave comrads! charge the foe,"
Good Heaven! it was a glorious sight
  To see those plumes stoop low,
And the serried men with fear again
  Back in their fortress go.

Rode by his General on a steed
  That snuff'd the fight afar,
And swallowed the ground at each furious bound,
  And said 'mid the trumps, "ha! ha!"
While the field all round his reeking path
  Blushed like Aceldama.

Out spake old "Rough and Ready" then,—
  "Burst on them through the wall,"—
'Twas answered by a deaf'ning roar,
  And the thundering cannon ball,
And a crash, as when a thousand oaks
  In a lonely forest fall.

Then he heard a mighty shout go up,
  Like the voice of myriad waves,
"Ho! Mexique soldiers fill the breach,
  Or be forever slaves!"
And the death wind like a tempest blast,
  Tore the banners off their staves.

But the hurricane rushed on amain,—
  They fled like driven leaves,
While fort and tower fell crumbling down,
  As when an earthquake heaves,
And the men who guarded them were "swept
  Like icicles" from their eaves.

Yet still at the head of his hand, he led
  Their steps where a foe might seem,
And his crimson sword in the seething smoke
  Flam'd like a lightning gleam;—
Till, anon, a thunderous roll of drums
  Shook the battle of his dream.

A shout! and the dreamer knew full well
  'Twas the children of the Free
That were hurling their cry through the shatter'd sky,
  To the God of Victory,—
And his soul had well nigh burst its chain,
  In its triumphant glee.

A change swept over the sleeper's brow:—
  He weened not of space between
The battle-field and his pleasant home,—
  The Gulf and the mighty Stream
And thousands of miles had all been pass'd
  In the whirlwind of his dream.

The homestead smiled in the pleasant light
  Of a sweet September morn,—
He could hear the crush of the reaper's hands
  Amid the golden corn,
"Be still, distracting thoughts," he cried,
  "Of war's mad folly born."

His Parents stood at open door,
  Their words were few and meek,
He tried to tell of the glorious fight,
  But his lips refused to speak!
And now like a burning seal they lay
  Upon his sister's cheek.

Oh, wealth of Love! what charm hath fame?
  That men make mock of thee,—
He would not have given that moment's joy
  For a tenfold victory;—
But hark! young soldier, the spell is broke,
  'Tis the drum beats Reveille.

He woke—Historic page will tell
    What glorious deeds were done,—
But woe for the dreamer! he hath no part
    Beneath the golden sun.—
Oh! weep for that brave young friend of ours,
    Who a soldier's grave hath won.

Maury County, Nov. 9.

From the Academist.

ON THE DEATH OF CAPTAIN WILLIAM B. ALLEN.

At Monterey—as the soldier joys to die,
The flag of his country, waving o'er him high,
The gallant ALLEN fell on the battle plain,
Where laurels were dyed in dark crimson stain;
Where shouts of victory on the free breeze floats,
And cheers of triumph swell, 'midst wild war notes,
Foremost there, in fight among that gallant band,
Young ALLEN fell—the pride of his native land.

He fell as the soldier—and calm be his rest,
With green laurels crowned—by his country blest—
And old age, and manhood, will echo his fame,
Repeating the valliant and much cherished name,
Whilst the spirit of youth, like a charger spurred
By the clarion's swell—at the glorious word,
Will be thristling for honor, and spurning at fear,
And bounding to follow young ALLEN's career.

He died, upon the ensanguined battle plain,
Where laurels are freshened with dark crimson rain,
Where the loud rolling drum, and the fife's shrill tone,
Nerves the soldier to stifle the low death groan,
Where the clasp of the soldier's cold hand, thrill,
And bid the heart leap, ere its pulses are still,

Where no message of love, from him can be borne,
To fond parents, who never will greet his return.

He fell, where the war-cloud was gathering fast,
Where havoc, and horror, were borne on the blast—
Where he led, valliant hearts—the hero of the hour,
The eagle's broad pinions, in pride, and in power,
Leading onward—amidst the cannon's dread rattle,
Leading onward—forward, the foremost in battle,
He falls, as a soldier of liberty—he dies,
And angels attend his spirit to the skies;
For sure, the martyr of freedom, is given
A glance of the future, when ripe for Heaven.

 October 30, 1846.   ROLAND.

From the Academist.

LINES ON THE DEATH OF CAPT. WM. B. ALLEN,

AND HIS COMRADES, WHO FELL AT THE CAPTURE OF MONTEREY.

The sun that rose on Montery,
 Ne'er looked upon a band more brave—
When Tennessee's bold chivalry
 Reared high our banner, there to wave;
Amid the dreadful battle din,
 Undaunted moved the Spartan few,
To wear the wreaths that valor win,
 They onward to the conflict flow.

Young Allen, with his sword on high,
 His hero band to the conflict leads,
Each noble bosom in emotion vie—
 In patriot fervor—and in valiant deeds.
Where fiercest raged the battle storm,
 The youthful hero, with his fearless band,

Appears in front—his manly form
   'The gathering tempest to withstand.

No nobler spirit in the bosom burns,
   Or warms to action the gallant brave,
Than that which base dishonor spurns,
   And rushes on to glory's grave.
The gallant Allen thus inspired,
   His trusty comrades by his side,
By lofty love of country fired,
   On glory's altar nobly died.

Onward, still on, they bravely press'd,
   To win the meed of high renown—
And as the noble warrior's crest
   Was mingling with its laurel crown,
Their gallant leader low was laid,
   But even in death's brief agony,
"He shook on high his battle blade,
   And shouted, 'onward,' 'victory.'"

                    OLO.

From the Times.

STANZAS,

TO THE MEMORY OF THE LATE CAPTAIN WILLIAM B. ALLEN,

WHO FELL AT THE BATTLE OF MONTEREY.

Alas! we mourn the silent dead,
   For those we weep the silent tear,
And the sweetest one is always shed
   Upon the gallant young soldier's bier.

And Allen's name long shall blaze
   High on his country's brightest page,

And be the honest theme and praise,
 Of the patriot and sage.

And the Poet, like gems around it,
 His greenest lays shall twine,
And the trump of fame shall sound it,
 Down the burning track of time.

When he heard the war horn cry,
 As it rang through city and field,
Soon his manly form he did supply
 With his father's sword and shield.

Then he bravely left his childhood's home,
 And the scene of his youthful prime,
And crossed the roaring ocean foam,
 To "do or die" in a distant clime.

And when the desperate charge was made,
 Where vengeance rode each ball and shell,
He flashed on high his battle blade,
 And in the first ranks fighting, fell.

But of complaint not a single word
 E'er escaped his fast fleeting breath,
He only firmer held his trusty blade,   .
 As he calmly slept in death.

He fell alone on a foreign shore,
 Where he was by no kindred blest.
And his country' flag covered him o'er,
 And victory's shout bore him to rest.

There many a gallant deed was done,
 And many a daring spirit laid low,
But few a greener wreath have won,
 Than that which binds his brow.

But no more in the golden morn,
 When the lights of memory burn,

Shall he heed the sounding bugle horn,
  And to the battle-field return.

No more shall San Juan's yellow wave,
  At midnight hour his funeral dirge be,
Friendship has wrought him a prouder grave
  In the sunny land of the free.

There he may lie and sweetly sleep,
  His deeds all done but not forgot,
While love his early doom shall weep,
  And fancy immortalize the spot.

Boon's Hill, 1847.   PHILAZMA.

LINES,

IN MEMORY OF CAPT. WM. B. ALLEN, WHO FELL AT MONTEREY—

SON OF GEN. R. H. ALLEN, OF LAWRENCE COUNTY, TENN.

When the fierce battle-cry was heard
  Upon the far-famed Rio Grande,
Where the base Mexicans had dared
  To set their foot on Freedom's land;
The brave young Allen was among
  The first who cried, "To arms! lets go,
We must defend our country's wrong,
  Drive back the insolent Mexican foe."
He was his father's pride and boast;
  His mother's dearest, fondest hope—
Those who best knew him loved him most,
  The favorite of the household group.
He had just began life's grand career,
  His course was like a brilliant star—
When of his country's wrongs did hear,

H

He hastened to the seat of war;
  The Lawrence boys chose him chief,
    To lead them on at Monterey—
"Brave boys," said he, "I'll be your chief,
    Then on to death or victory."
He then girt on his sword and said:
    "This is the sword my father gave—
It shall be honored till I'm dead,
    It has ne'er been worn but by the brave."
And when the mighty conflict came,
    There was brave Allen with his band.
In the front of battle, winning fame,
    By valorous deeds, with daring hand;
Just as the foe was put to flight,
    The fatal ball then ends my story—
Young Allen fell in glorious fight,
    He sleeps in death, all crowned with glory.
Aberdeen, Dec. 20, 1846.

FLORENCE, Alabama, Oct. 12, 1852.

GEN. R. H. ALLEN—*Dear Sir:* Herewith enclosed
you will please find the hasty and imperfect editorial
tribute, which I paid to the memory of your dear, departed son, through the columns of my paper, the *Florence Gazette.* The death of your son has often impressed
me with sad and melancholy reflections. He had, I believe, just finished a collegiate education. He was fresh
from the Legislative Halls of his native State. His
mighty heart beat "high and warm," and in the language of England's great Bard, life seemed a "banquet,
a song and a dance." He was the soul of chivalry.—

His majestic form was as tall and stately as the strong oak, while his beaming countenance gave an unerring reflex to the kindness, goodness and sweetness which swelled his noble bosom. Thus he left his "aged parents"—the ease and comfort of a happy home, full of lusty life. His heart was filled with sanguine expectations, and deeds of noble emulation. Under the streaming folds of his country's banner, he marched forth amid the fiery torrent. The iron grape that grew in such fatal clusters and so luxuriantly on the hill-sides of Monterey was poured upon him, but he blenched not.—His fiery young heart seemed stirred to courageous madness, as his comrades fell by his side, and he rushed on with impetuous madness: But, alas! alas!! just as the enemy was vanquished, and the trumpet shout of victory was heard, your poor boy received a mortal wound, and his red blood mingled with his neighbors. It was then

"Hope for a season bade the world farewell,
And freedom shrieked a requium as he fell."

Methinks I see the young brave now, as he lay prostrate upon the stricken field which his own valor had already won. As he lay breathing out his heart-stricken soul, gush after gush, the earthquake voice of victory filled his ears, and as he proudly turned his dying gaze upon the triumphant stars and stripes, he made one faint effort to shout *"victory!"* but his great heart fluttered, and his soul winged its flight to eternity.

"His countrymen wept, that in life's brightest bloom,
One gifted so highly should sink to the tomb;
For in ardor he led in the van of the host,
And fell like a soldier—*he died at his post.*

He wept not himself that his warfare was done—
The battle was fought and the victory won;
But he whisper'd to those that his heart clung to most
Tell my countrymen that *I died at my post.*
He ask'd not a stone to be sculptur'd in verse;
He ask'd not that fame his merits should rehearse;
But he asked as a boon, when he gave up the ghost,
That his friends might know how he *died at his post.*"

For the death of your son, the tears of the nation fell fast and free; but they flow rather for the living than the dead—for the nation that has lost such a patriot, for you and for the heart-broken *mother.* For *these,* we weep tears, bitter, heart-felt tears; but not for your gallaut boy, for we rather envy his enviable fate. He fulfilled the highest destiny man owes to the world—*he died for his country.* I know that in the person of your son was garnered up all the treasure of your affections. To him you looked as the solace of your declining years, and his untimely death has no doubt sorely lacerated and bruised your bosom. It is a chrushing stroke, and I presume that neither your philosophy or your manhood can repress the sad sigh, or stifle the falling tears; but I trust you will in some degree be consoled by the reflection that a grateful nation has already inscribed the name of WILLIAM B. ALLEN upon its annals, and long after you and I have passed off to the "silent land of the sleepers," and taken up our abode in the "silent city of the dead," his name will be cherished fresh and green in the hearts of his countrymen. I believe, in the quiet seclusion of your own garden rests the remains of your gallant son, and as you repair at twilight eve, amid singing birds and blooming flowers, to pay homage to his memory, you can point to the monument which lifts its tail spear to the skies, and say in the language

of the Roman mother as she held up her children—
"*These—these are my jewels.*" These reflections have,
I may say, almost involuntarily suggested themselves to
my mind in contemplating the death of your son. I
write them hurriedly, without time for reflection or re-
vision, you will therefore excuse all inaccuracies. With
my best wishes for your happiness, I remain

Very respectfully, your friend,

M. C. GALLAWAY.

From the Florence, (Ala.) Gazette, Nov. 7, 1846.

THE DEATH OF WILLIAM B. ALLEN.

While the whole nation is rejoicing over the triumph
which perched upon our banner in the recent battle at
Monterey, the heart of the patriot almost involuntarily
turns from its rejoicing, to mingle its tears over the
graves of those who fell. The fall of WILLIAM B. AL-
LEN, of the Tennessee Volunteers, has evoked the universal sorrow of the American people. His fate is a
melancholy one. It affords another exemplification of
the old old adage, that "death loves a shing mark"—
that the brightest and best, the youthful and beautiful
are the objects at which the relentless monster ever aims
his unerring arrows. Just in the bloom of manhood—
fresh from his College studies and from the halls of his
State Legislature—with his young breast swelling with
a thousand dreams which the young alone can weave—
of patriotism, ambition, love and hope—he has fallen on
the battle-field, on a bleak and foreign strand, and has
brought mourning upon his venerable parents.

When a call was made for Volunteers, Capt. Allen organized a brave and chivalrous band of patriots. Their
country only beckoned, and these magnanimous sons

thronged to enlist themselves beneath the broad folds of
her glorious standard.   They rallied to the rescue, and
while young Allen was gallantly leading on his brave
men, and nobly driving back the cohorts of oppression—
the mercenary hirelings of despotism, he, with many of
his spartan band, fell.   Just as the proud flag of his
country was about to wave in triumph over the field of
battle, he fell

"Gloriously fighting in a glorious cause."

He was buried with all the honors of war, in the
midst of the tears of his fellow-soldiers.   It is said no
cowardly fear blenched his manly cheek.   He knew his
end, and departed without a murmur, and with an abi-
ding confidence in the mercy and goodness of his Re-
deemer.   He went thither at the requisition of his God,
and as a soldier for Eternity.   He has, ere this, answered
to the new *roll-call*, and we believe his patriotism and
his goodness will give him a peaceful parole in Heaven.
Light rest the turf on his bosom!   The genius of his
country will guard the spot hallowed by the remains of
the patriot that has died in her cause.   Let us pay his
memory that homage worthy the great cause in which
he fell.   Let the youth of the country repair around his
grave as around the shrines of liberty, to catch the fire
of inspiration, and as they pass the green turf that rises
over his slumbering form, let them exclaim in the ful-
ness of their hearts:—

"This shall resist the empire of decay,
When time is o'er, and worlds have passed away;
Cold in the dust his perished heart may lie,
But that which warmed it once will never die."

Although Capt. Allen fell in a distant land, his friends have the consolation of knowing that his remains are now quietly resting in the County of Lawrence.—The following account of the ceremonies which took place when his remains reached home and were interred, will be found deeply interesting :

From the Lawrenceburg Times.

HONOR TO THE BRAVE—THE FUNERAL.

On Saturday last, the remains of the late Captain WILLIAM B. ALLEN arrived at his father's residence, from Monterey, Mexico. Yesterday, about a thousand of his friends and acquaintances assembled to commit his body to the tomb. The day being fair and pleasant, a very large number of ladies were present. The body of the gallant dead was soldered up in a leaden coffin, within another of mahogany, on which a large silver plate, bearing the name of the deceased, was fastened.

Hundreds were there, who about nine months since, took leave at the same place of the friend they had now met to bury. They remembered, and often remarked the contrast between this and that assemblage. Then, with buoyant feelings and brilliant hopes, the brave Allen left his home at the call of his country; they saw him depart with pride and pleasure. Now, they met in sorrow, to mingle their tears with those of a large and respectable circle of his friends and relatives. We have never attended any funeral where there was such general and deep sorrow depicted in the countenances of the spectators.

The order of procession to the grave was, as near as we can recollect, as follows: *The Hearse with Military escorts, attended by Music on each flank. The Relatives*

*The Clergy. The Monument Committee. The Ladies.—
The Citizens.*

The fine volunteer company from Mt. Pleasant, commanded by Capt. Alexander Terry, with such part of Col. Tarkington's Clay Guards as could be hastily assembled, formed the escort. The whole conducted by the Marshal of the day and his associates, S. E. Rose, A. S. Alexander, A. O. Richardson, and Thomas C. Ramsey. The two last gallant youths were the observed of all observers, having each lost an arm at the assault on Monterey.

At the grave the usual ceremonies took place, with military honors. We believe that notwithstanding the great number of persons assembled with carriages and horses, such was the order and decorum preserved, that not the slightest accident occurred.

At the close of the ceremonies, Chief Marshal, S. E. Rose, Esq., delivered the sword of Capt. Wm. B. Allen to his father, Gen. R. H. Allen, accompanied by a few appropriate remarks, that exhibited his power and eloquence. We have seldom, if ever, listened to a more touching, a more eloquent discourse.

The following is the beautiful Address made by Mr. Rose on this melancholy occasion:—

MR. ROSE'S ADDRESS.

LADIES AND GENTLEMEN:—I have been honored to-day with wearing the *sword* of WILLIAM B. ALLEN.—Language would fail to portray my feelings, or express the deep emotions of my heart. I received this sword with the pride of a soldier, and I wear it with the devotion of a friend. Yes, this goodly sword, with which the gallant Allen has written his name upon the tablets

of immortal memory, and engraven it upon the columns
of the temple of fame—methinks I can see in imagination, this Sword in the heat and front of the battle—
there it flashed, the harbinger of victory. Yes, gallant
hero, well hast thou made thy pledge to thy father true,
"That this sword should never be dishonored." It has
returned not dishonored, but wreathed with immortal
laurels—aye, decked with the gem that valor wins.—
What a sublime picture the mind draws of this youthful hero with his gallant band, rushing on midst the
thickest of the fight, to glory and to victory:

> Onward—still on—they nobly pressed,
>   To win the meed of high renown,
> And as the noble warrior's crest
>   Was blending with his laurel crown,
> The gallant Allen low was laid;
>   But e'en in death's brief agony,
> He shook on high *this* battle blade,
>   And shouted, "Onward!" "Victory!"

But he is no more. He is dead, yet he lives—lives
in the memory of his countrymen, cherished in the affections of all who knew him. Though his manly form
lies low in death, his many virtues, his towering talents,
his brilliant example, shall continue to abide in the
memory of the living. The history of his short but
brilliant career shall be the theme of the orator, and be
sung in numbers of the patriot bard. But we have
come to bury, not to praise him. He needs no eulogy;
his name shall brighten with the lapse of years, and
grow brighter as centuries roll on.

He left the endearments of home—the hallowed
scenes of his early remembrance—father, mother, brothers, sisters, all, to fight the battles of his country in a

distant land, where he fell, without a relative to mourn his untimely fall, or hold his dying head. But no more shall the night winds of that hostile clime sing his sad requiem—no more shall San Juan sigh her melancholy lullaby to his departed spirit—no more shall the rude chapparel wave its sombre branches over the fallen brave: for Leon has given up her dead, and friendship's hand has borne him far back to his native home, to be re-embosomed in the silent grave—where a mother's tears will bedew the sod that covers his last remains ; where the prayers of his father shall make vocal the air that encircles his lowly bed ; where brothers, sisters, friends, shall, from the deep fountains of the heart, their grateful tribute of compassion pay—

> And friendship thy tomb shall rear,
>   Since glory thou hast won ;
> And Freedom's self shall hover near,
>   To weep her fallen son."

Venerable sir: I now return to you the sword of your gallant son. It will go down in your family as a sacred heirloom, and posterity shall hold it in the high estima- tion it so richly deserves.

In the same gallant company in which Capt. Allen en- listed as a volunteer, his younger brother, SAM. Hous- TON ALLEN also enlisted. He too, was destined to die far away from his home. When the venerable parents of these two intrepid young men bid them farewell, and gave them their parting blessings, as they left their homes to fight for the honor of their country, they little thought that they were taking a long, last farwell. It remains now for the writer to bring this sketch to a close.

by a brief reference to the life and character of the younger Allen.

He was born in Giles county, Tennessee. on the 9th of October, 1828. When he enlisted for the Mexican War he was less than eighteen years of age. Actuated by the same noble patriotism which animated the bosom of his gallant brother, he determined to take the chances of war by his side. Until they arrived at Camargo, they were inseperable companions. At this point, Sam Houston Allen was attacked by the prevailing disease which carried off so many of our brave troops. When the forces were ordered to advance on Monterey, he was too feeble to bear the toil and labor of the march, and he was amongst the number of those who were honorably discharged on account of sickness. He returned to New Orleans on his way homeward, but at that place his symptoms became worse, and finally his disease proved fatal. He died on the 26th of October, 1846.— Whilst lingering on his sick bed at New Orleans, he received the distressing intelligence of the death of his brother. When the news was communicated to him, he said: "I would rather have died than to have heard that news. Oh! that I had not been taken sick and had been by his side; I would rather have fallen with my brother than to have died any other death." These feeling expressions show the warmth of the attachment which existed between these two noble brothers. Like his brother, Sam Houston was a model of virtue and morality, and like him he was prepared for death, being an exemplary member of the Cumberland Presbyterian Church, as was also his brother. This fact sheds a brightness over their tombs, and furnishes a substantial comfort to their friends.

CHAPTER IX.

The Monument erected in Lawrenceburg—The Funereal Sermon of the Rev. P. P. Neely.

THE high estimate placed upon the heroic conduct of Capt. Allen and his brave associates who fell at Monterey, has been manifested by the erection of a beautiful Monument, on the public square of Lawrenceburg.— This lasting testimonial was the result of the generous, voluntary contributions of friends, who wished to exhibit their admiration of the gallant dead by some permanent memorial which should show to future generations, how warmly they admired true patriotism and chivalry.

On the 15th of August, 1847, the Rev. P. P. Neely delivered the Funeral Sermon, on the death of the two young Allens, which is replete with that splendid eloquence for which that distinguished divine is so celebrated. At the request of many of the friends of the deceased, he furnished a copy for publication, and it furnishes a proper conclusion to this imperfect sketch.

FUNERAL SERMON

Pronounced at MOUNT ARARAT CAMP-GROUND, *Lawrence County, Tenn., August the 15th, 1847, on the occasion of the death of*

CAPTAIN WILLIAM B. ALLEN,

WHO FELL AT THE CHARGE OF MONTEREY.
BY REV. P. P. NEELY, D. D.

"He being dead yet speaketh"—Heb. 11 ch., 4 v.

We are assembled, my countrymen, upon an occasion of melancholy interest. We meet to-day to pay a tribute of respect to the memory of the young and the brave who have fallen like the beauty of Israel, in the high places of our country. I need not announce the names of those whose early immolation of themselves upon the altar of their country, has filled so many eyes with weeping, and bosoms with desolation. They are graven 'on the hearts that beat in this multitude, with an indellibleness which the flight of years, and the gathering of sorrows will never efface. I feel that I cannot do justice to my task. It is one from which I shrink, and would have withdrawn myself, but for the earnest solicitation of one, whose paternal heart bleeds, as memory lingers amid the carnage and death of Monterey. Around me are congregated on this occasion, the weeping constituency of our departed young friend: those who had invoked him from the retirement of the paternal roof, whither he had gone to indulge the warm affections of his filial heart, so soon as he was released from his collegiate toil, and casting upon him their voluntary suffrage, bade him go forth, and be their organ in the legislative councils of the State. These are here. I see before me many who were with him in his early boyhood: who were partners in his sports—companions in his rambles, and whose memories of him, embrace a thousand tender associations of youth, which cannot enter the recollections of the more aged; you too are here, to weep, as we bid you gaze on the pale form of your early boy-associate—shrouded and dead.

Here too, are those who realize a still deeper sympathy--a sadder grief--his soldier boys. These went forth to do battle under his banner. They were his companions amid the fatiguing march,—they slept by his side upon the same cold earth--gazed with him upon the same blue covering, and like him, thought of loved and absent ones. *They* have listened to his kind words around the distant camp-fire, and when sick, have been tended by his hands, and fed from his own soldier's platter. They were with him too, amid the din and peril of battle—heard his deep voice as it rose above the thunder of death, encouraging them on to valor and to victory.— They saw him, when in the pride of youth, he fell, covered with glory, and what is better, prepared to meet his God. *You* are here, and in your bosoms must exist emotions to which we are strangers.

And yet, others are here, whose unuttered grief is too deep to be alleviated by earthly balm. We would willingly invade the sanctuary of your hearts, if we could hope by it to dispel the gloom, by the casting of one gleam of sunshine there. Your holiest consolation will be, that your country has received at your hands, the richest offering you could bestow—the priceless jewels of your love—and heaven has had its songs augmented by tones that once tremblingly addressed you as *Father* and as *Mother*.

Surrounded thus, my countrymen, I cannot but realize the magnitude of the duty imposed upon me. I feel, too, that the occasion is one that must enter with peculiar strength and earnestness into the hearts of many that compose this mighty multitude. In meditating upon the character of those whose lives we are called upon to notice, you can but remember an analogous loss which you have sustained : memory will cause to pass before you the familiar form of some one, dear to you, as the subjects of this day's assemblage were dear to their kindred, whose bones moulder in a distant soil, and whose lonely sepulchre is unvisited by friends, and unwatered by the tear of affection. Deem not yourselves excluded from what little consolation we may be able to offer. We came as a people, at the appointment of the friends of the deceased, to offer our condolence especially to them : yet they claim no monopoly. We have sympathy for all, and would tender it to all. Seeing too, as we have good hope that it is so, that the spirits of your sainted soldier-boys are rejoicing together, in the enjoyment of eternal peace on high, we, their friends, met to dwell upon the virtues of their brave leader, would extend to you our warmest sympathies in your bereavement, and our most sincere prayer for grace to sustain you in their endurance.

It were needless for me to say that I rank myself with pride among the warm friends of WILLIAM B. ALLEN! for who is there among this vast number, that were honored with his acquaintance, but can give truthful expression to the same sentiment? I must be indulged, when I say to you, that during the twelve months' intimacy I maintained with him in the metropolis of our State, I realized a friendship, the growth of which has never been equaled toward any other in so short a time. I loved him—deeply loved him—and have met you, his old friends, his schoolmates, his soldiers and his kindred, to recall his virtues, to dwell upon his brief, but glorious career, and to gather from it lessons of encouragement in performing the destinies we may have to meet in coming years.

We come with no pomp or pageant to-day; such would little become the occasion. The ground upon which we meet is too holy, and the purpose in view too high, to have its mournful solemnity and impressive awe disturbed by the roll of a drum, or the thunder of cannon. We come, not so much to do honor to the soldier, who has ceased from his toils and entered upon his rest, as to seize upon the spotless name he has bequeathed us, and holding it up before our young countrymen, invoke them to emulate an example so adorned with integrity, so radiant with glory. It was right, that the stars of his country's glory, and the stripes upon which he gazed amid the cloud of battle, should wave over his bier, when they were about committing his returned dust to the soil of that country for whose rights his heart had been stilled. The muffled drum, the mournful music, the nodding plume, the soldier's tears, all comprised a pageant in keeping with the task to be performed—the placing in the bosom of our mother earth one of her bravest soldier sons; but meeting now to commemorate those traits that beautified his life, and encircled him in his departing hours, with a halo of imperishable glory, such pomp and circumstances may well be dismissed.

One of the early customs of the Romans, was to fill their halls with the images of such of their families as had rendered themselves illustrious. These images consisted of masks representing the features of the dead, with the costume worn by them—their armor, and various insignia of their position among men, and the glory they had won. These were so placed around the ancestral hall as to convey the appearance of living men—so that the descendant had constantly before him the regular succession of his ancestry. Upon the death of any member of the family, of distinction, a wild and fanciful procession occurred. These ancestral masks, costumes, armor, &c., were placed upon the servants of the household, who, arranged in the order of succession, followed the newly deceased to the market-place, where a eulogy was pronounced over him, and from thence they repaired to the tomb to commit his body to the sepulchre of his fathers. The effect of this awful cavalcade was overpowering. The young Roman, as he gazed upon the dark ancestral line, apparently animate and breathing, offered anew his vows of patriotism, and caught a fresh enkindlement of glory, as it leaped from the passing throng.

We are assembled, not to gaze on such an array of departed ones, not to look upon theatre representations like this, but to remember the patriotism of our brothers—to contemplate their services—to place in our hearts the beautiful memory of their goodness, and to realize the truth of our text, they *"being dead yet speaketh."*

Our object in your further detention, will be to impress upon you at once the idea in the text—viz: that the conduct of each actor on the great stage of life, is to influence mankind, after the release from among them, and then to enquire into the voices that steal upon us from the lives of the deceased.

Human existence, my hearers, must have its termination. We speak now of the suspension of the animal functions, and the realization of that change which leaves the eye closed upon the most beautiful objects, and the ear heavy to the sweetest melodies, and the heart dead to the tender emotions. We mean the period in the history of immortal man, when all that is visible of him to the natural eye, or tangible to the touch, is shut out from our view, and the grave opens her dark bosom, and folds her arms over us, in our forgetfulness and oblivion: when the pleasures that may have beclouded the soul: the schemes of ambition or of benevolence that may have engrossed the powers of the mind: the visions, on whose beautiful vestments we may have gazed, as they careered by, like the gorgeous cloud, moving in mid heaven upon its invisible wheels: we mean

I

the period when these, and all else that stirs the great multitude of mankind shall have passed away from our contemplation, and we shall have entered upon another state, to be engrossed by the mighty scenes to which the present bids us look. In this sense *all must* DIE. The doom hangs on all, and has passed upon all, with a few exceptions, from the hour in which the knell of heaven proclaimed, "dust thou art, and unto dust shalt thou return:" and so will it continue until that period shall have arrived, to the full display of which John was admitted, when he "heard a voice out of Heaven, saying, there shall be no more death." This however, is but the dweller from earth—but the veiling of his face from the living, while his actions remain to bless with their good, or curse with their evil. God has so established it, that the agitations we give birth to, while voyaging the sea of life, are to march on with a dominant and widening sweep—gathering strength in their ample circlings—until the dirge of time's last wave breaking upon the shore of eternity, shall be lost amid the voices that people the endless future.

It is a solemn and unalterable fact. It has upon it the fiat of heaven, and no disaffection on our part can change it, no striving to hide ourselves in the shadow of obscurity, will avail in excluding us from its awful application. We are here, in existence, composed too, of indistructible elements: endowed with a being on which the seal of immortality has been set. No mortal power, no hand waving in the dominions of the damned can break that seal. Obscurity of birth or of fortune cannot lift it from us, nor can the darkness of the sepulcher dim its lustre. God has placed it upon us, and there it must forever remain. The law of our being—the law of society—the great law of influence is, that actions live after the actor dies. In this sense we are all architects, rearing piles on which coming generations will gaze, when the names of their builders shall have perished amid the unremembered past. We are all casting for ourselves mementoes of glory or of shame. These may be different, as there may exist a disparity in our means of doing good, or diffusing evil; one may be a massive base, surmounted by a turning shaft on which the eyes of multitudes—of the world—may rest, while others may modestly lift themselves from the family altar, visible only to the throng of devout worshippers that kneel at its peaceful shrine; yet are we all—rich and poor, old and young—artificers in action, building for all time—building for all eternity.— These mementoes of ourselves, so invisibly preparing, are to stand as our representatives—as instruments of blessing or of cursing to the world—when our names shall be effaced from the vast catalogue of the living.— We will perish amid our labor: the clamor of the builders—the revel, the shout, may cease—all memorials of our individual names may be lost; still our actions—our undying actions—will be seen, radiant with increasing glory, or shrouded in darkening shame.

Oh! think not that life is so bound up in isolated selfishness, that we can enter upon it and continue in it without contributing our part—great or little, as we may have opportunity—to the rolling of the vast population of which we are part and parcel, toward that perfectibility sung of by the herald of a golden age, and disclosed to us in the brighter revealments of prophecy, or else of heaping upon its massive wheels leaden weights of obstruction.

We are here, and must act in some way, and every deed has inscribed upon it ETERNITY. Life is but one great registry, where each dweller is entering his deeds. These are to be read by succeeding ones, and are to influence them; and ultimately this volume is to be inspected at the grand assize of heaven, and by its contents destinies are to be rewarded.

The doctrine which we are striving to impress upon you on this solemn occasion, is forcibly illustrated by the entire history of mankind. We see the seal of one age, with more or less of reality in impression, resting upon the succeeding one. The events of a generation cast their outline upon that which follows. There may be, there always are, distinctions marking a difference in each, yet the shadows or the sunshine of the departing, will rest with distinctness upon the dawning one. The mighty events that distinguish an age, (and what are events but matured action?) often form the elements of a revolution in that which follows. To this doctrine of reproducing influence, are we to attribute the success which crowned the struggles of our fathers in the cause of freedom, and the subsequent achievements of the American people, which have made them second to no nation in the world. The intolerance manifested toward the Puritans, prepared them for the course of stern resolve, which resulted in the settlement of New England, and finally in the existence of this free nation. The incredible privations endured by them from an oppressive hierarchy, wrought in their souls a hatred for tyranny and a love of freedom. Upon this aliment they fed their sons and their daughters: and rearing these in the free, wild solitudes of America, where the green earth and the vaulted sky were crowded with symbols of freedom, no marvel that its altar was the great colonial heart, and that when she demanded it, each hardy descendant was willing to yield as his offering, his own warm blood.— Our free institutions, founded upon and supported hy the principles of republicanism, having upon their front the high seal of prosperity and of national glory, and receiving too, the homage of the friends of liberty everywhere, proclaim the might of the influence of that generation; yea, farther, the universal throbbing of the heart of freedom, beginning to be felt, from the classic plains of Greece, to the farthest range of the distant Cordilleras— even to the sun-visited plains of Yucatan—shout in trumpet-tones of the majesty of that influence.

Nor is it less true with regard to the revolution by which ecclesiastical powers have been shaken. Seizing upon but one, for the sake of illustration—the Lutheran reformation—behold what a moral change suddenly passed upon the world, through the influence of one master-spirit, and the actions of one generation. A fearful darkness had settled upon the religious world, and extended its effects to the civil powers. Man was sunk in the scale of being: fear tyrannized over the passions, and reason was bound in the chains of passion. Brutal, lawless lust, and greedy ambition trod the earth with a dominant step, and science, honor, virtue, patriotism and devotion were fogrotten, and every right, human and divine, was disregarded. An awful night had cast its pall over the world, and darkness, unmitigated by the beam of a single star, seemed to hold the world spell-bound.— "Science became empiricism, and the pure religion of the Prince of Peace itself, became the pander for the lust of power and wealth, and was made the instrument of crushing to the earth the very beings it was designed to elevate.''

Thus hung in clouds and impregnated with storms, the darkened firmament was made bright by a solitary star that was hung out in the middle of the fourteenth century. During the fifteenth and sixteenth, others were visible, and in the sixteenth the German Reformer startled the world by the lustre which he shed around him. Since that period light has been increasing. Luminary after luminary has appeared, sparkling groups have burst forth, and now the retiring darkness—the beautiful light not only visible upon the hill-tops, but coming down almost from mid-heaven itself—is a witness of the power and increase of its influence.

What has been affirmed with regard to generations, may with equal truth be appled to individuals. There is not one of the actors that throng the mighty stage of life, but who when the drama closes, leaves an impress on the vast platform. The memory of the head of the houshold throng lingers long with the sorrowing remnant: and often in distant years from the sad event that made the child an orphan, memory comes, with its sad, lute-like tones, from the wreck which profligacy may have heaped upon it, and whispers to him of the past Oh! it is in that hour of bitter reminiscence that the ghosts of murdered blessings, of violated innocence, and of destroyed peace, are invoked from the past, and the deep piety of that mother, the godly conversation of that father whose efforts to bring back the prodigal were unavailing in life, gathered as it were from the grave, snatched from the lives of those who once lived, tell with emphasis the influence exerted after death, and prove that the dead speak with a voice that breaks not from the lips of the living. Who does not now, while we speak, bring from the cells of memory the form, the look, the words, the life, and even the death, of some dear departed friend or relation.

The grave, it is true, holds their dust, but their lives are with you still. Their pious words; their fervent prayers; their devotional songs; their last sickness, with its suffering and patience; their closing hour, with contest and triumph; all are yours to dwell upon, and from them to gather consolation to do, and strength to endure, whatever in the providence of God may be needful for you. Holy lights they are, that burn beautifully bright in the sepulchre of the past, pencilling with their beams the truth, that the dead speak. Innumerable are the voices that steal up from the burial-grounds of earth.-- The dead, all the dead—the dead everywhere—pour forth the oratory of the charnel house. The rude resting place of the humble cottager, and the pompous mausoleum of the prince, are alike vocal. The gorgeous sarcophagus, in which the scion of royalty sleeps, and the unsightly ditch, where the poor beggar found a release from his suffering, send up a kindred eloquence. The dead all speak. I would earnestly impress this upon the living, that they may so live, as that from their dust a voice may arise, the tones of which will cheer some pilgrim on his lonely way. We repeat it then, the dead all speak. Not even the solemn chime—the knell of their departure —can drown their tones; neither the cold clay, nor the green earth, in whose bosom they await the resurrection, can muffle them: their voices come in the wild revel, in the giddy dance, the lonely hour, the sabbath stillness, the twilight's hush, the midnight's awe, they come: from earth and from ocean, they send out their pealing

tones, proclaiming that though dead, they yet speak.—
We may dismiss them from our sight, yet we cannot consign their deeds to forgetfulness. If their lives were
made up of actions worthy to be admired, these deeds
"can never die, nor dying be forgotten." Indeed it
would not be deemed enthusiasm to say, that at death
they just begin to live—they just enter then, upon that
existence of mighty influence and unclouded fame here,
and of uninterrupted bliss there, for which their devotion
to their country, to humanity, and to their God, so pre-
eminently fitted them. Those whose lives dwell not so
much in the physical as in the mental and moral world:
whose steadfast hearts never slumbered: whose souls
struggled up into a nobler being: the great end of whose
efforts was to do good: whose riches consisted in a name
without spot: whose intrepidity was displayed in daring
to do right: whose spirits were interposed in the institutions of their country and of the church: whose names
have been engraven upon her proud pillars, and the
blood of whose brave hearts has been poured forth in her
defence—such men were not born to die: no cloud of
death can hide them from our view: no veil of dark se-
pulture can shut them out.

Go tread the solemn height of Bunker Hill. Gaze upon the marble shaft, pointing to the high empyrean above,
and tell me if the deeds of a Warren, who fell there in the
infancy of our national existence are forgotten. While
that pillar braves its summit to the tempest, or receives
the dew which heaven distils upon that holy ground, will
the actions of that brave officer and his martyr band be
fresh in the hearts of his countrymen. Tell me, ye who
visit the shades of Vernon, is Washington confined to the
little vault in which his body was laid? Is there no-

thing left of him but the indistinguishable ashes that
people a narrow house of earth, guarded by a few bending willows, and dirged by the ceaseless roll of the Poto-
mac? Has Monticello, which contains the hand that
penned the charter of American Independence, monopo-
lized all that is left of a Jefferson? and say ye who knew
him in the quietude of peace, and in the terror of battle
too, has the lion heart of a Jackson no mightier boundary than the republican vault at the Hermitage? have
those impulses which stirred his soul—so patriotic in
their intention, and so iron-like in their execution--gone
down into eternal silence with the noble dust they animated? No, no!

> These shall resist the empire of decay
> When time is o'er, and worlds have pass'd away:
> Cold in the dust the perished heart may lie,
> But that which warmed it once can never die.

Oh! there is a beauty, a majesty in the thoughts connected with this theme which we must give vent to.
The framers of our constitution! the archives of our independence! the preservers of all we hold dear as freemen, gone, but still remembered. The lips that were
eloquent in our defence, when the word liberty was
treason, have become silent: the arms that did battle for
us have become dust, and the hearts that offered their
blood have perished; still their spirits are with us. Their
actions, embodying all that was noble in patriotism and
lovely in virtue—evincing an utter abandonment of all
self, an absorption of all interests and all purposes in the
holy one of their country, are our legacy. Blessed in-
heritance! to these our satcheled school boys turn for
examples worthy of emulation. These are beacon-fires,

lighting up the sea of state amid our heaviest calamities and darkest hours; these, rising upon the coast, become pledges of safety and harbingers of success.

We may rear the marble pile, and bring the undecaying brass to preserve memorials of them, but images more vivid, and monuments more lasting than these, meet the gaze every where. Their country—their happy country—their whole happy country is their eloquent attestor of their virtues. The humblest mound of earth, rising over the brave dead, in our free land, arrayed in its robe of sunshine, and glittering in the dew-drops of morning, is a prouder mausoleum than royal oppressor ever reared o'er their tyrannized herd. Our country, we repeat, is the monument of her deliverers. Their epitaph is her freedom. Glorious names! not only have they broken the chain thrown upon their own nation, but the victims of old despotism hear them and give indications of life. And thus will it be until the wild pulsations of the world's heart be for liberty. Whenever an agonizing people shall perish in a generous convulsion for the want of a valiant arm and fearless heart, they will cry in the last accents of despair, oh for a Washington, a Jefferson, a Jackson. "Whenever a regenerated nation starting up in its might, shall burst the links of steel that enchain it, the praise of our venerated fathers shall be the prelude to their triumphal song."— They being dead yet speak.

Seeing then, my beloved hearers, that we are to leave an impress upon the sands of life when we are called from its busy pursuits, how deeply should we be impressed with the solemn importance of passing upon our conduct a constant and rigid scrutiny. Of what immense moment is it to us, and to those who are to live after us,

and who are to be moulded, to some extent, by the influence we are to leave behind us, that we study to make
that influence profitable. When we die, we too shall
speak from our tombs; the sound will arise either to glad-
den or sadden the then living; we will then have sent
upon society a breath that will either fan into life, or
wither into death, the beautiful buddings of moral virtue.
Which will you do? you cannot be nutral: there is no
such ground for your occupancy; your life will be vocal
with lessons of good or evil, of virtue or of vice, long after the grave will have closed over your clay. We invoke a decision this day. That you may be stimulated
to a wise choice, we proceed now to lay before you a
brief synopsis of the lives of the brothers Allen, who,
united in life, were scarce separated in death.

Having consumed much of the time allotted us already, we cannot enter into a particular detail in the performance of this mournful task. Passing rapidly over
this part of our sad duty, we shall strive to present such
traits as were most conspicuous, and should most excite
your emulation.

With Samuel Houston Allen we had not the pleasure
of an acquaintance, which must serve as an apology for
not alluding more frequently and particularly to him.—
He was born Oct. 9th, 1829, and was in his 18th year
when he died. From a few documents which has been
furnished us. we learn that all that was dutiful in a son,
modest in a youth, generous and faithful in a friend,
were impersonated in the life and conduct of this interesting young man. To these traits of character many that
hear me now can bear witness. You knew him in early
boyhood—the period of life when the fountain of action
is without the fetters which a better acquaintance with

the world throws upon it.   You shared an intimacy with him at an age when the conduct is without a mask, and knew well the nobleness of his nature.

After reaching the seat of war, finding his health broken so as utterly to unfit him for duty, and not wishing to burden the army without being effective, he consented to receive an honorable discharge from the service.   He had proceeded as far as the city of New Orleans, on his return home, when disease invaded the citadel of life; and he who had gone forth full of hope, yielded his spirit to God who gave it.

There was much that was feelingly touching in the closing of this young man's mortal career.   Our sympathies are all drawn out as we contemplate his death-scene: he was far from home, and surrounded by strange faces. Had he been called to meet death on the field of battle, it would have been far more enviable.   There is something in such a death that renders the spirit terribly fearless.   The war of artillery—the thunder of cannon—the clash of steel—the tramp of cavalry—the streaming of banners, like thunder clouds against the winds of heaven —the dauntless words of the dying—the vision of future glory to our country, breaking upon the failing eyes of the pale soldier, as with gaze fixed upon the moving symbols of that country, he passes far beyond the milky baldric of the skies, to a dominion in which no voice of war is ever heard—all contribute to throw around the pale horse and his skeleton rider, a glorious enthusiasm that renders him a welcome messenger to the stalwart warrior.

He feels, as life gently drops its veil, and all things are shut out from him, that posterity will enroll his name among the bright catalogue of immortal martyrs; and

thus cheered by the voice of fame, he dies as brave soldiers ever die—mocking the power of the monster. Oh!
there is about such a departure, a wild, burning enthusiasm, which however impotent in preparing to endure
throughout that awful eternity which is to follow, divests
death of its terror, and girds the dying with a rainbow
of glory.

> Thus die the brave, who sink to rest
> With all their country's wishes blest.

But to linger day by day in an enfeebling contest with
the destroyer—to look in vain for the familiar faces
gazed upon in childhood, or the yearning look of love
that bent over our cradle in watchful solicitude in the
helplessness and innocence of infancy—to hear no brother's voice, or sister's tones, breaking with hope and
encouragement upon the leaden ear, as death gradually
seals it to all earthly sounds. To have nothing but visions of home and its dear ones, its remembered spots and
unforgotten things passing before us, without hope of
ever again mingling with them around the board, or altar
of prayer. To die alone, or with strangers, and to feel
that we must sleep with strange companions, is to *me*,
indeed, a destiny, the vesture of which is full of melancholy—one too which can only be alleviated by the reflection, that over these, religion can display her brightest
manifestations, and administer her holiest consolations—
the sweeter, perhaps, because of the absence of all human comfort. Such was the death of Samuel Houston
Allen, and such the consolations he received.

His death couch was not surrounded by a venerated
father or a beloved mother, yet the God and Father of
all was there to give him strength. No faithful brother

or loving sister hung over him, to wipe from his brow
the grave's clammy dew; yet blessed be God, Jesus
Christ, his elder brother, and ministering angels, soon
to be his companions, among whom perhaps, was his brother William, were near, and mysteriously strengthened him in that hour of awful struggle

Thus died our young brother—a christian by profession and by practice—a nobleman by nature, and a martyr to his country by providence. We mourn his departure
in humble resignation to the will of Him who hath taken
him. We "mourn not as those without hope," for although the spot that contains his body is not known to
us, still God marks it, and in his holy keeping it is safe.
Yes,

> God his Redeemer lives,
> And ever from the skies
> Looks down and watches o'er his dust
> Till he shall bid it rise.

With William Bethel Allen our acquaintance was
more extended. A necessarily brief biography will now
claim your attention. He was born in Giles county,
State of Tennessee, the 16th of Jan. 1824. His childhood was passed under the eyes of his parents: and if
it be true that domestic education moulds the future
man, his father and his mother deserve the highest
praise for that course of early training pursued with
their son. Rich indeed must be the reward they have
already shared in the honorable race run by their sons,
and in its peaceful, though early termination. May their
example not be lost upon the guardians of the rising generation. At the age of 16, William entered Haliden Hill
Academy, under the superintendence of Mr. W. W.
Potter, whose fervidly eloquent sketch of the life of the

deceased, we have had the pleasure of perusing. The worthy principal of that institution has awarded him the highest character as a diligent student, an obedient pupil, and an humble christian. It was there that he laid the groundwork of that ripe scholarship that he ultimately attained, and of that warm eloquence of the soul that so frequently enchained listening multitudes, and which reflects praise alike upon his own untiring industry, and upon the qualifications of his preceptors.

Having completed the course of study preparatory to his matriculation at college, he entered the Nashville University, under the presidency of that remarkable and accomplished scholar, Rev. Dr. Lindsley.

During his connection with this Institution, we made his acquaintance. We but speak what is personal knowledge when we say, that he had a devotion to books, reaching almost to idolatry, and a zeal the most burning : an ambition, which, while it aimed at the highest achievements, had none of the meagre elements of envy or jealousy in it—seeking his own elevation, and wishing the while to forward that of others also: a piety whose amply laid, and profoundly cherished principles, preserved him from the corruptions attendant upon our large cities, and made him a lovely example of religiously fortified virtue, towering above vice, and gathering strength amid surrounding corruption—together with a friendship which was blind to all selfishness, and more than "argus eyed" to the interest of those who shared it—these were the leading qualities that fired his mind and warmed his heart. What we have said is fully sustained by the following deserved compliment paid him by the learned President of the University, a man whose praise is never bestowed but when merited. "This ex-

cellent young man graduated in 1844, having been connected with the University three years, during which
time he received the entire confidence, and heighest esteem of the faculty and students—he was uniformly the
example and advocate of every thing that is lovely and
of good report.

Having passed the regular term, and completed the
prescribed course of studies in that Institution, he received from the proper authority the honors he had won,
and bid adieu to his beloved Alma Mater, his honored
preceptors and his cherished class mates, and sought the
endearments of sweet home and waiting firiends.

You remember my countrymen—for you were his
neighbors—the plain simplicity that marked his manners
upon his return. In some instances, the tendency of
University associations—city intercourse—fashionable
mingling, &c., is to create in the mind of the young man,
whose college ambition was, not so much to enrich his
mind with endearing wisdom, as to enjoy these—a false
conviction of self importance—an arrogant assumption of
superiority to which he can lay no claim, and which converts him into a contemptible coxcomb, instead of one
worthy to be an example.

Such however cannot be affirmed of young Allen.—
He met you as he had ever done. *He* affected no city
exquisitism, but with a friendly smile and a warm grasp,
he showed that whatever of knowledge he had accumulated from books, it had not been gained at the sacrifice
of that simplicity of manner which ought ever to characterize true republicanism.

His continuance at home was but short; for he had
just but received the greetings of kindred and friends,
before the partiality of the latter placed him before the

people as a candidate for a seat in the State Legislature. The field was new to him, and doubtless but little congenial to his wishes, yet ever prompt to do service when invoked to it, he yielded his consent, and entered upon the stormy sea of politics, upon which so many gallant young men have been ruined for time and wrecked for eternity. The same integrity of character, conscientious adherence to truth, and respect for those of diverse sentiments which had distinguished him in youth, and won so many warm admirers, were still exhibited.

Fearless in his defence of the political tenets honestly entertained by him; prompt and bold in their vindication, he never lost sight of the fact, a conviction of which should be settled upon all disputants, that his opponents had equal claims to sincerity with himself, and should therefore be respected. As an evidence of the exalted esteem in which he was held by his fellow-citizens, he was chosen by them to represent their interests in the councils of the State when he was barely eligible, and that too over a competitor of extensive popularity, and whose long service and faithful discharge of trust in the Legislature of his State, had made him emphatically the man of the people.

As a Legislator, his course was such as to meet the universal approval of his constituency, upon his return to their midst. His position in that body, for strength of intellect, valuable information, and clearness of debate, would have been an honor to a head silvered with age. His unbending probity secured for him the confidence of both parties, while his youthful appearance and commanding eloquence won for him the rapt attention of the waiting crowd.

J

Soon after his return from the session of the Legislature, another voice broke upon his ear—it was the voice of his outraged country, whose rights had long been disregarded by an ill-judging foe, and whose soil had been invaded by that foe. It was the voice of his periled countrymen, who were menaced by indiscriminate massacre, from superior numbers. The cry which came upon the rushing wind, from our little band of regulars, stationed with their gallant old leader Gen. Taylor—the living Jackson in the present military age—startled him from the quietude of home and the endearments of friends. It fanned into a conflagration the flame of patriotism that had long been gradually kindling upon his heart, and in common with many of his early associates, the brave sons of his old neighbors, he came forward as a private, and added his name to the list of regular soldiers furnished by your chivalrous country. In companionship with these he left you. We will not dwell upon that farewell. Let memory turn from it, for it hath too much of sadness in it; and to array before you that departing column, would be to lift from the past too many blighted flowers that perished from that hour.

Such was his popularity, that soon after he reached Mexico he was chosen by the company—with whose fortunes he had united his as a common soldier—to command them. In his conduct as commander of his company, we see exemplified the nobleness of his nature and the benevolence of his heart. He claimed no superior privileges, no exemptions not awarded the common soldier. What *he* had belonged to all who labored and suffered with him. His devotion to them was superior to all selfishness. As an instance, we would refer to his declination of the office of Quarter Master, tendered him by President Polk. Writing to his father, under date of 14th of Sept. 1846, he says, "I have this day sent my resignation to the President who appointed me Quarter Master. The boys are unwilling to be commanded by any one else. By the grace of God, I will try to lead them without dishonor, to victory." What affection for his company ! What devotion to his God ! In another letter, written during the prevalence of much sickness among his troops, he says, "I have thirty-five or forty of my original company who are still able to march with us. They feel like brothers. I regret to leave those behind who are on beds of affliction. I hope they will soon rejoin their friends. May the great God protect and support them in all their trials and afflictions."

These attachments were not the offering of the occasion, so much as the natural yearnings of a soul great in its affections. Love of home and its kindred dwellers, and of friends tried and true, was a part of the man.— To give illustrations of this, we must be permitted to make another extract from his correspondence. Writing to his parents, he says, "I have been to Point Isabel twice, for the purpose of getting a letter or paper from home, without success. My anxiety to hear from you is as great as is the distance which separates us from each other. I would be willing to deprive myself of every other earthly possession for the sake of seeing my relations and friends. Never before have I been capable of duly appreciating the pleasures of home. Here *we* are, upon an inhospitable and desert island. For us no rainbow smiles are wreathed, no hallowed invocation offered.— But for those who are *far* away, and who live, and will ever live in our affections—for them we have forsaken the endearments of home, for them we are willing to fight, or for them we are willing to die. Whether we return home in time, or fall in the field of battle, I hope that a good report will animate us ever afterwards, or cheer our friends when we are no more."

These extracts show to us the patriotism by which he was incited—the filial affection he possessed, and the christian confidence he maintained.

We approach now, the last act in the eventful drama of his short life—the storming of Monterey and his untimely death—and how can we dwell upon it? True it is a part of his history, in which we behold a convergement of the rays of glory, which had been beaming from him in increasing majesty from his early boyhood? Yet in the midst of it he fell, and no breaking light can make us insensible of the sad truth, that it is but the gorgeous garniture of the mourned—the beloved dead. The attraction of that hour, great though it be, cannot divert us from a contemplation of our loss; and the achievements won in it, can never warm into life the noble hearts that then became cold.

The day ultimately dawned—a day, the coming of which had been waited for with feverish impatience by the American forces, the day that was to try their unfledged swords, and afford opportunity for gathering immortal laurels, and avenging the blood of their countrymen that cried unto them from Palo Alto and Resaca de la Palma. They had hoped for it long, and had kept vigil with the fleeting hours the night before, so eager were they for its arrival. It dawned at last. Glittering in the distance might be seen the spires of Monterey—calm in the beautiful sunlight that slept upon them—unconscious too, of the awful carnage of which they were to be silent witnesses before that sun should go down. Behind dark fortifications, that frowned as if the scowl of war was upon them, were placed those messengers of death—the deep mouthed cannon, those murderous dogs of war—waiting to be let slip, that they might bowl the requiem of the departing ghosts of the soldier multitude. There was the deep entrenchment below, and the walled height above, from which protruded dark implements of death.

The busy hum, swelling from the warrior men—glittering bayonets—gleaming swords—waiving plumes—columns of infantry—lines of cavalry—the pealing drum—the piercing fife—the voice of command—all tell of a mighty preparation for the work of death. At length they come. The flower of Tennessee are in the van. Lovely sons! would that the doom that hung over many of you in that hour of elation could have been averted! No! no! The altar is prepared, and ye were to be the offering. Ye were the precious jewels of more than Spartan mothers, and they sent ye forth, consenting to the sacrifice. Oh! America! America! thou art ever glorious whilst thou canst boast such mothers as these. Silently, yet with determined step, that van-column marched on to certain death. Is there no quivering of muscles? Is there no paling of the cheek—nor convulsive trembling of lip? There may have been, when the tread of the moving host just started, sounded like a sepulchral blast, but now there is none. Sometimes perhaps, as memory repaired to the circle of home, and returned with the tears of a mother or a sister shed upon their departure, and held them before the soldier boy, his heart may have beat with wild emotions: yet one thought of his country —his mother—would calm the tumult, and change him from the son into the soldier. At length the *charge* is

pealed along the line.   Amid the wild rush of armed
men—the heaps of slain—and the falling wounded that
yielded before the raking fire of the enemy—behold your
son—your former citizen—your brave leader, with lifted
sword—the same whose steel, when received from the
hands of his honored father, he had breathed a vow never
to dishonor it, and with the voice of the roused and fearless lion, encouraging his followers on to the breech, and
on to victory, until struck by a cannon ball, he fell! Nor
does the scene of his earthly glory close here: for grasping his sword with the fervor of death, and looking for
the last time upon his wasted column, he exclaims "*Boys
I am dying, but charge the fort,*" thus mingling with the
last gleam of earthly light, the noble principle that guided him through life—*patriotic even in death*—"*I am
dying but charge the fort.*

"Life's parting beams were in his eye,
Life's closing accents on his tongue,
When round him pealing to the sky
    The shout of victory rung!

When e're his gallant spirit fled,
A smile so bright illumined his face—
Oh! never of the light it shed
    Shall memory lose a trace.

His was a death, whose rapture high
Transcended all that life could yield;
His warmest prayer was so to die
    On the red battle field.

And may they feel, who loved him most,
A pride so holy and so pure—
Fate hath no power o're those who boast,
    A treasure thus secure."

Such was the life and such the death of William B. Allen, a man than whom if God ever made a nobler, *we* never knew them. His life was an examplification of patriotism--his death the commanding seal affixed to it: and can ye dream that one so rarely gifted—so entirely his country's and his God's; and so early called from the service of one to be companionship with the other, can repose in the grave, in forgotten oblivion? or that no voice will ascend from his dust—no mighty swell from his memory? No! though dead, he speaks to us to day. Though corruption has claimed his mortal part, his immortal deeds are ours--ours to cherish and ours to imitate. People of Lawrence! Freemen of his native State! he has bequeathed you a legacy richer than all your vast possessions--his own illustrious example. Oh value your heritage. Impart it to your babes as you gather them around the warm fire for winter evening communings. In coming years, as your sons visit the neighboring town, and see an unadorned column rising from the earth, tell them of the spotless life—tell them of the glorious death of him in commemoration of whom it will have been reared. Tell them of his affection for his parents--his love of knowledge—his regard for morals —his devotion to his country--his fidelity to his God— tell them *all*—and as you send them forth, bid them mould themselves by what William B. Allen was.

Glad am I, that his bones have been gathered from a foreign soil, and placed where the tread of a foe can never insult them. The heart of his own proud State is a sepulchre worthy of him. Upon her green turf he trod when a child, and it is right that that turf should cover his clay. Here the emotions of his heart were first quickened, and then matured; and it is well that that heart

should repose here when it became still.   He sleeps in
your midst.   The grave of his childhood has become his
warrior couch, guarded by the affection of his father and
the love of his mother.

> "Rest warrior! rest! by the father's hand
> Thither shall the child of after years be led,
> With his humble offering, silently to stand
> In the hushed presence of the glorious dead,
> So rest! warrior! rest! for thou thy path hast trod
>   With glory and with God."

Young men of Tennessee!   Soldiers whom he led to
victory, to you he still speaks.   He calls you by all that
is lovely in virtue––by all that was of good report in his
conduct, and that was glorious in his death, to be emu-
lous of doing good to your God and to your country.

He is not with you now––he is gone.   Strive in the
great battle of life to keep his example before you, so
that its close may be marked by equal triumph.   Kindred of my dear young friends? Father! Mother!
though gone they speak to you.   They address you from
the past.   Their warm affection, uniform obedience, and
kind words, speak consolation to you in your tears.
They speak to you from their heavenly abode.   Beautiful voices steal down out of heaven to cheer you now.
They whisper of the departed.   They tell you of the
temple in which they dwell, and of which, in a little time
you are to become occupants––of the waiving fruit––the
glad river––the blessed songs––the waiting friends––they
tell you of heaven, and bid you be ready to scale the
inaccessible heights, and share those joys forever more.
Speak on! beloved ones! we hear your distant voices and
hope soon to see you as you are, and so be ever with the
Lord.   . PHIL. P. NEELY.

Columbia, Tenn., Aug. 8th, 1847.

APPENDIX.

SPEECHES AND ESSAYS,

By CAPTAIN WM. B. ALLEN.

A SPEECH, DELIVERED IN THE PRESIDENTIAL CAMPAIGN OF 1844.

Fellow-citizens:—A period is approaching, in the history of our country, of no ordinary interest and concern. A battle is now being fought, bravely and earnestly, that is to settle for years to come, the questions at issue between the parties. It is gratifying to me to observe with what enthusiasm and fire the democracy have been fighting this battle. Although instances are on record of men entering a contest with fearlessness of spirit and burning zeal, whose ardor was damped and energy weakened before it was over, it is a cheering fact, that so far as the democracy are concerned, not one single feather has been plucked from their caps, and by their unanimity and assistance, the contest will wax warmer and warmer until victory, joyous victory, will crown their efforts, and our long cherished principles be restored to their natural position. Although I have been so circumstanced that I could participate but seldom in the exultations which have gone up to heaven from the proud hearts of freemen, I have nevertheless, been privileged occasionally to attend most of their numerous meetings, and united with them in their patriotic rejoicings. The country is all on fire—it burns brilliantly and gloriously all over the land—and right here where the people ought to be free from the curses of corporated establishments and the imposition of oppressive burthens —here in hearing of our distinguished leader who is to lead us on to victory, let the clarion voice of the democracy be heard longer and loudest. Let the people from the adjoining States hear it, and let them raise the shout and echo it from hill to hill, from hovel to hovel, until nought else will be heard but the exultation of the unterrified democracy. Shall this be the case my countrymen? Shall leagued oppression ever gain the ascendency in this country? Every voice is ready to exclaim it shall never be—every heart swells the anthem and exclaims forbid it Heaven! Let the ball then in this contest be kept rolling, and let no one despair of success. I believe the people in Tennessee are firmly united, and genuine, sterling democrats. The people have been divided by following different favorites, some of whom have made a ship-wreck of their political faith. Who does not well remember the time when we were all united in supporting zealously, and harmoniously, and unanimously, the administration of the immortal Jackson? We were all one under his banner. We supported him not only for his patriotism, but we agreed with him in the measures which characterized his administration. How have the people become estranged from him? How have they forsaken their old principles, which they were once willing and ready

to make any sacrifice to mantain? I ask the candid,
honest whig to ask himself this single, isolated question.
Can you reconcile your present course by your former?
You who supported through State pride or through
principle, Judge White, a man no less distinguished for
his honest patriotism, than his eminent abilities as a
statesman, and believing him at the same time to be, in
every respect, a better Jackson man than Mr. Vau
Buren, would do well to examine the causes of your
opposition to the democratic party? In your zeal for
Judge White's promotion, did you agree with him in
principle? If so, how does it happen you are in favor
of a National Bank by federal authority, and a protective
tariff, measures to which he is well know to have been
hostile from a consideration of his public acts in the
Senate of the United States and elsewhere? You can-
onize his memory and profess to have unlimited confidence in his judgment, yet you oppose the essential
measures which characterized the whole course of his
public acts. Whence this change? Whence this glar-
ing, palpable inconsistency? Have the people changed?
Upon what principles pray? Were there any acknowledged party division drawn upon the faith of principle
in that contest which rent in twain the republicans of
Tennessee? There were none, absolutely none. I
appeal to history and experience for the truthfulness of
this asseveration. You were then Southern men, having
southern interests to succor and protect, and Tennessee,
proud and chivalrous as she then was, stood as one man,
contending zealously and indefatigably and patriotically
against Banking corporations and the duties on foreign
goods beyond the requisite amount to defray the
economical expenditures of the government. This was

the doctrine held, in all sincerity, by the wise, disinterested patriots and war-worn veterans of our revolution, whose blood flowed out in fountains to redeem their country from the curses of British taxation.   And now, after having made several experiments without sufficient cause of a repetition, we are again called upon to support such an institution, as, in my humble estimation comes directly in conflict with the best interests of the country, as it certainly does destroy that horizontal equalization which forms the basis of our Government.   That it is a lucrative business to a few individuals who possess a little capital and invest it in Bank Stock, is quite certain. But that it benefits at large the whole American people, in all their varied interests and dealings, would be an admission unauthorised by evidence and unfounded in truth.   The fate of the late Bank, with all its crimes of commission and omission, is known too well to require an attentive review now.   That it was not strictly speaking a Bank of the United States of the removal of the deposits, may be admitted, as it is admitted, without at once invalidating the conclusions we have drawn, for the United States Bank of Pennsylvania, as it was called, was not altered in any of its important features from its primitive form, and Mr. Biddle, himself, the President of the Bank, declared the State Bank was on a surer basis than before the stock of the Government had been removed.   But why speak of this measure?   We are to speak of the living and not the dead.   The Bank question, is now, "to all intents and purposes" an obsolete idea.   If not, why do not its favorites and advocates make it the absorbing question in this canvass, as they certainly did in 1840?   The only reason I can assign, is, that the times wont justify it.   Under the pressure of pecuniary embarrassment, thousands of honest men were induced to vote for such an institution as a relief measure, as they thought, but finding now that relief is making its appearance without any such artificial agencies, they are unwilling to be deceived longer. Every man knows that exchanges are better than they generally were during the existence of the Bank. These and many other considerations, have, no doubt induced the whigs to consign that question "to the tombs of the Capulets." The next subterfuge of the party is the Tariff. They tell the people that it is politic and expedient for our Government to protect home industry against foreign industry. But whom do they propose to protect? Is it the honest farmer who cultivates the soil? Is it the hard-working man who has settled him a home in the west, where he hopes to settle his children upon comfortable and suitable farms? Is it the man who has him a home in the bosom of the forest as it were, that this shield is to cover? No sir. It's the manufacturer who asks and implores Congress to give him this advantage. What does he ask it for? Is it that he may sell his articles cheaper? This would be the worst of folly. If I understand them, the foreigners undersell them, and they want the tariff that they may realize higher prices. And who pays the money? It's the hard-fisted farmer who has never implored Congress importunately and repeatedly for protection in his line of business, that has to pay it. If industry is to be protected at all, it does seem to me that it should be done in all its branches. Or as our leader says, "It is the duty of the Government to extend, as far as it may be practical to do so, by its revenue laws and all other means within its power, fair and just protection to all the great interests of the Union, embracing agriculture, manufactures, the mechanic arts, commerce, and navigation." We are told that it is British and not American goods we are taxing. Well if by taxing English we could make them pay for it, I would go with you in that measure, but when we examine the matter we find we are taxing British goods and making ourselves pay for it—"that's the rub." The money comes out of our own pockets not Englishmen's.

A few more words and I have done. It is scarcely necessary that I should speak of the cheering prospects that smile upon our efforts in the cause in which we are engaged. Wherever an issue has been made by the unbought expression of the people's will, the democracy has done nobly. The merited frowns of a people indignant at past injuries are resting upon those who, by their acts, are endeavoring to change this Republic into a Consolidated Government. The spirit of our patriot fathers rise up from their graves and condemn it. Upon the preservation of the "social compact" depends, in a great measure, the perpetuity and happiness of the whole country. The man that advocates consolidationism on the one hand, or disunion on the other, is ignobly base, and deserves the universal hatred of mankind. However much men may be disposed to differ in opinion upon subjects connected with the administration of government, upon one thing they do agree—that this Union must be preserved at every peril. He that anticipates and wishes its dismemberment is not worthy, in the least degree, of enjoying those favored blessings Providence has spread so profusely about us. He deserves to spend a miserable existence in some dark, cheerless abode, where Heaven's free sun never flings

his radiant smiles. When such a factious, disorganizing
spirit is once aroused, (and which may Heaven merci-
fully avert,) the depository of all our dearest hopes and
brightest anticipations is assailed, and the strong arms
and stout hearts of our citizens may not be able to
quell it. In all our eagerness to support men we should
always keep an eye single to our country, for what is the
elevation or depression of any man when compared with
her preservation, perpetuity and happiness? If men
prove false to those interests entrusted to their care—if
they are guilty of a flagrant and open violation of those
pledges upon the faith of which they are promoted to
office—if they become negligent and careless about
adhering strictly and faithfully to the "letter and spirit
of the constitution," they should not only be watched
with a zealous and suspicious eye, but hurled headlong
from their high places, into the deep den of infamy and
disgrace, which, I must confess, has been the recipient of
a smaller number than justice demands. Men may be
boisterous and noisy about their patriotism and fidelity,
but we should examine with care their acts, for by their
acts ye shall know them. Men should be nothing, and
principles everything. Upon this maxim the fathers of
the constitution acted. If we are ever so recreant to
our trust, as to support men zealously, without any
regard to the measures they would be most likely to
carry out, and in so doing our system of equality is
destroyed by a latitudinarian construction of the constitution on the part of those receiving our favors, the
greatest curses that could rest upon a people will hang
like angry clouds about us. Men's opinions must be
known, that he that runs may understand them. Any
doctrine that infringes upon the rights of the humblest

citizen of the country, ought to be discarded, for although it operates advantageously to one class, it proves to be prejudicial to the other. No patriot could wish these favors, when he is told that others entitled to the same protection from government are groaning under its oppression. If there be any beauty or excellence in our Government, every individual under its fostering wing takes part of the honor to himself. If it should prove a curse to us, in the name of fairness, let us all, not a few—but let us all partake of its evils. If the vessel of State, with all its stars and stripes is to strike a quicksand, and to be scattered in dishonored and disorganized fragments upon the buffetting waves, I for one, am willing to share the fate of the crew on board, let it be what it may. But we should be cautious in getting a pilot and helmsman to guide us in safety from the rocks. He should be cold, calculating, prudent—a cool head and stout heart, with the circumspection of command and an invincible will that can say to the waves, "peace be still," and the storm ceases. He that possesses an oversweeping ambition that swells into proud insolence when irritated by casual disappointment, is dangerous to be trusted with such an important charge, for like Phæton, who overturned the chariot of the sun, and sat the world on fire, he may overturn the vessel at his discretion. But such a spirit will be hurled from his seat not by Jupiter's thunderbolt, but by the omnipotency of the people's will. The man we are willing to be our leader possesses none of these dangerous qualities—he is an honest man—"the noblest work of God." He has stood by his country in the darkest period of her history, and never forsook her. He has fought and done battle nobly in defence of that pyramid of principle erected as the

proudest monument of the wisdom of our ancestors.—
By its side he has professed a willingness to stand, or
fall at the solid base upon which the superstructure is
reared, with the stars and stripes of his country winding
around him. He is one of those concurring fully in the
opinion expressed by Mr. Jefferson, that the "mass of
mankind had not been born with saddles on their backs,
nor a favored few booted and spurred ready to ride them
legitimately by the grace of God." He is in favor of an
equal distribution of justice to all—special privileges to
none. He wants the government to extend its sovereign
arm of protection around all of its citizens. He believes,
as he has expressed it, that "it is the duty of the government to extend, as far as may be practicable to do so,
by its revenue laws, and all other means within its power,
fair and just protection to all the great interests of the
Union, embracing agriculture, manufactures, the mechanic arts, commerce and navigation." Here is a
statesman for you, whose heart is as large as the whole
country—whose wishes are to encourage all departments
of human industry by all fair and efficient agency of the
government. How nobly and honorably do his views
contrast with his opponent's, who avows that "agriculture needs no protection?" But I leave this and similar
questions to be decided by the great American people.
The time is not far distant when these things will be settled beyond a doubt. The battle is to be fought upon
principle. You who believe in the measures which were
held to be sacred by the sterling patriots who framed
the Constitution, are invited, as you are exhorted, to
rally to the support of Polk, Dallas, Texas, Oregon and
the Constitution. Judging from the recent indications
which have developed themselves in the State elections

K

which are just over, we have high and gratifying assurances of triumphant victory on the first Monday of November next. In every instance where an issue has been made by the people, our cause has been sustained by increased numbers who have said in their might, they will stand by it or fall with it. When men who have filled a large space in the public eye, are daily divesting themselves of habiliments of whiggery, may we not reasonably infer that thousands and scores, not so prominent, though equally honest, will in the face of all the evidences which truth can afford, renounce allegiance to the party that has proved recreant to the many solemn pledges they so earnestly made, and so willingly and probably conscientiously disregarded? The waters are being moved and agitated. The tide of popular indignation is rising high against those who have been wafted into favor upon its powerful current, and now threatens with little or no hape of avoiding it, to overwhelm those who have enjoyed the luxury of riding upon its majestic bosom. Truly may it be said, the way of the transgressor is hard. Who, under the weight of the astounding weight given already by the people, can anticipate anything like certainty for the success of whiggery.— Has not State after State, in unbroken line, fixed a seal of condemnation upon the great embodiment, that he might deceive the nations no longer. And as sure as the presidential election shall roll round, a shout such as was never heard before, will arise from every section of the Union, proclaiming that Babylon the great has fallen. Along the length and breadth of our land, will burst the shouts of triumph. The people's artillery, bloodless though condemnatory, will thunder forth the deafening notes that "we have met the enemy and they are ours."

Then, then fellow-citizens, will these inquisitorial, party-serving, editorial scribblers, know to their infinite sorrow and mortification, who James K. Polk is?

> "Closed is the brunt of the glorious fight,
> And the day, like a conquerer, bursts on the night,
> Trumpet and fife, swelling choral along,
> The triumph already sweeps marching in song."

Do your duty, democrats, and there is no cause for fear. That you will do that, I have not the least doubt. Tennessee must and will be redeemed. March up then to the election, with a determination to loose no honorable means on your part to secure that result. In the contest which is nearly over, be firm and immovable, never for a moment forgetting that "our principles are our shield, justice our sword, and our battlements are the hearts of the people."

A SPEECH ON THE ANNEXATION OF TEXAS.

Fellow Citizens:—Our Constitution and laws guarantee to every citizen of the United States, protection from injury and a continuation of equal favors. He that is raised in a splendid mansion "whose lofty tops ambient clouds conceal," or in the most indifferent hovel, situated in some bleak solitary waste, exults in the consciousness that this government will ever throw around him the broad, impenetrable ægis of its protection. He knows the objects for which governments were instituted, and considers himself an integral part of its machinery. To secure these blessings arising from an uninterrupted enjoyment of conscious security, the torch of the revolution was lit, and this fair land enveloped in one general conflagration. For this our fathers barred their bosoms to the storms of a seven years war. For this they fronted with unrelenting firmness the British Commons, and bid defiance to its deafening thunders. For this they dissolved all connection with the mother country, forming a Constitution of their own. For the maintenance of our rights, the second war of our Independence was fought, which has illumined with a blaze of glory the history of Tennessee chivalry. Some of the invincible sons of Tennessee, animated by no other zeal than intense patriotism, prompted by no other motives but to render useful service to their country, shouldered their muskets and marched to the plains of New Orleans, and made their own bosoms a breastwork to the enemy.— The battle was won, peace was restored, and their hearts beat rapturous joy. After performing these feats of noble daring, after having conquered the pride of the British army, they crossed the Sabine, and settled their homes where they fancied to spend the remainder of their lives. They expected that the wounds they had received in battle would be healed, and never again be exposed to the application of the sabre and sword. But how infinite their surprise, how intense their mortification, how distressed their looks must have been, when they received the intelligence that by the treaty of 1819, they had been sold to the Spanish monarch. Was not the United States bound to protect them, by its Constitution? Had they not a right to expect it? And yet, from a free government, by unwise negotiation, they had been transferred to a monarchy, against which, on a former occasion, they had freely offered their lives.— This is not all, my countrymen. They submitted their unjust treatment in a manner becoming their conditions. But soon the Spanish yoke became so galling that they were unwilling to bear it longer. The Mexican Revolution ensued, and these old soldiers, who had fought under Gen. Jackson at the battle of New Orleans, were again found on the side of liberty, fighting manfully for freedom. The result of that Revolution is well known. It is scarcely necessary to state, that the Mexicans were successful, and they, in 1824, formed what was called the Confederative system. The rights of the people were again insulted, and they were loudly called to redress the grievances. The military despot, Santa Anna, laid his iron grasp upon that system, and attempted and effected its dissolution. Texas peremptorily refused acquiescence with the other States, and she met, in proud triumph, the Dictator in the battle of San Ja-Jacinto, prostrating inevitably, all hope on the part of Mexico, to conquer and subjugate Texas. This was the third memorable battle in which these old soldiers had been engaged, in all of which they were found invariably on the side of liberty. And now, after having exhausted their treasure and their blood, with the seal of age fastened upon their infirmities, they ask in tones of impassioned eloquence, in cries of continued importunity, in the voice of justice and humanity, that the United States will receive them into that embrace from which they were unwillingly forced. Their pilgrimage in life is nearly ended, their wounds will soon cease to bleed, and their brave hearts cease to beat. They ask this not as a boon, but as a right; not in their own behalf, but in the name of their children, and their children's children. Who that is not lost to all sense of compassion and commiseration, can say that this desirable object shall not be obtained in consequence of a certain man's opposition to it, who wants to be President?

A SPEECH, DELIVERED AT THE JACKSON CELE-
BRATION, IN 1845.

Fellow-Citizens:—After the delivery of the very able
and eloquent address which you have this day heard, it
would be unpardonable presumption in me to attempt to
say much in addition. I feel myself incompetent to
succeed with effect, a man possessing such a store-house
of knowledge, such diversified and rich talent, and such
a vivid flowery imagination, as the distinguished orator
of the day. Our theme, vast as it is in extent, and interesting and marvelous, when portrayed in all the col-
ors of which it is susceptible, could not be exhausted in
the short space to which an address must necessarily be
limited. We have met here, on this the Sabbath-day of
Freedom—the Jubilee of our Independence—bringing
the offerings of grateful hearts, and depositing them
around the altar of our common country. The time and
circumstance under the auspices of which we have convened, conspire, eminently and supremely, to unite us
together in a community of feeling—to hush in the
silence of forgetfulness for a moment, the discordant
thunders which proceed from the bosom and angry fury
of a political storm—and to bury our local and section-
al prejudices and antipathies in the remembrance of the
past. We come together in the presence of the great
God of battles, whose omnipotent arm encircled and
shielded our patriot armies in the time that tried men's
souls, to commemorate the life and services of one of the
most distinguished men that this or any other age has
produced. Fathers, friends, countrymen, the great Jackson is no more! He whose name was once a terror to
invading armies, and at whose command our belligerant
forces were conducted to victory and to glory, has gone,

we trust, with the armies of the reedeemed, to a country
beyond the skies. The patriot and soldier, the statesman and the sage, at an advanced age, though full of
usefulness, has conquered the last enemy, death, and is
gathered with his fathers and compatriots in arms, in
the bright realms of fadeless, unwithering glory.—
If he has ever done wrong, as he undoubtedly has, let
them be buried with him. If he possessed virtues, and
he had many, let them be emblazoned high on the page
of history, let them be engraven on the tablets of
memory, and celebrated in song. Let the aspiring youth,
surrounded by the most difficult and trying scenes, look
with bright hopes to the example of Jackson. If he is
destitute of friends in the time of trial, let him remember that by acting well his part in life, he will finally
elicit the plaudits of admiring freemen. This dispensation of Providence also reminds us impressively and forcibly of the mutability of all human affairs—that no
station, however exhalted, exempts one from the summons that is to be made upon us all.

The question might be asked, why this parade—why
this demonstration of feeling? The answer is plain.—
We meet to pay suitable respect to the memory of him,
who came like the Roman general, saw and conquered
the enemy of our country.

> "Patriots have toils, and in their country's cause
> Bled nobly, and their deeds, as they deserve.
> Receive proud recompense. We give in charge
> Their names to the sweet lyre. The historic muse,
> Proud of her treasure, marches with it down
> To latest times; and sculpture, in her turn,
> Gives bond in stone and ever during brass,
> To guard them and immortalize her trust."

If monumental piles, and statues of marble and gold are being erected in honor of those distinguished for their wisdom, and renowned for their courage—if patriotism has erected its thousand altars to the skies, and genius bowed its head to receive the green laurels of fame, wreathed by the hands of its votaries, may we not at least give utterance to the language of our hearts, expressive of the estimation in which we hold the hero and sage, for his invincible bravery and exalted patriotism—for the undying blaze of glory he has shed around his country, by his statesman-like virtues and military prowess? To perpetuate his memory, and transmit it to all future time, there is required no storied urn—no monumental inscription. He yet lives in the hearts of the people, and his councils are not forgotten. His name has not and will not loose that potency with which it was invested in doing good. Yes,

> "When the storm of battle pours,
> And the invader's ruthless band,
> Fiercely on these western shores
> Seeks to conquer freedom's land,
> Sternly grappling with the foe,
> In the battle's redest flame,
> Where's the brave heart will not glow
> When we breathe old Jackson's name?"

He has lived long enough to see this the most flourishing nation on earth. Agriculture is advancing—Manufactures are springing into existence as by magic—Commerce spreads her canvass-wings upon every ocean—Internal Improvement is spreading its Briareus hands in every direction. Emphatically is this an age of improvement. Science, Argus-eyed, is erecting its hundreds of observatories, and extending its researches far and wide—Schools are springing up in every neighbor-hood, from which emanate the rays of intellectual light —the wilderness has been made to blossom, as a rose under seasonable and effectual cultivation—towns are strewing themselves all over the West—our people have been multiplied from three to twenty millions of souls—our sisterhood of States has been augmented from 13 to 29—Florida, Iowa and Texas, are members of the American family. Of a truth did Bishop Berkley say,

"Westward the course of empire takes its way."

But it is not our purpose to speak of the rapid devel-opments that have been made in the physical condition of the country. We are to speak of him for whom the nation is in weeds of mourning. He lived to an age to which but few have attained, and could look back to his boyhood to a well spent life. He has survived most of his compatriots and soldiers in arms who were engaged with him in defending our rights. A few yet remain among us. Yes, I see before me to-day, a remnant of that little band—that time worn fragment of the second war for Independence, who have met with us to pay suitable tribute of respect to their departed chief. Eter-nal be the remembrance of his fame, and peace to his manes! is the patriot's earnest prayer.

"The cause he espoused in his earliest youth,
  Is the star which led him to glory;
'Twas the cause of his country, of justice and truth,
  And his name shall illumin our story;
But ye demons incarnate whose hopes are all crushed,
  And whose prospects are blighted forever,
Your vile tongues are palsied, your slanders are hushed,
  And the hero shines brighter than ever."

If in a long life of brilliant usefulness, he has ever acted improperly when invested with the ensigns of office, it was in view of his country's glory; if he stood proudly at his post of duty, in defiance of the opposition with which he had to contend, it was because circumstances rendered it necessary; if he ever acted the part of a tyrant, of which he has been wantonly accused, it was that you might be free. From his boyhood to the time of his death, his exertions were used in opposition to oppression, in any of its protean forms or disguises. But it is not necessary that I should say any thing by way of eulogy upon that eminently distinguished man. His fame is co-extensive with civilization itself, and his virtues are written upon the tablets of memory, which the waters of Lethe cannot efface. His looks and actions I shall never forget while memory holds its sceptre. I saw him at his home—to which strangers resort to see him of whom they have heard. I saw him not as a conquerer, returning from the field of carnage with his garments dyed in the blood of the slain—not as an orator, at whose impassioned appeals assembly burst forth in spontaneous plaudits—not with the civic wreathe around his aged brow as it once was, but as an humble citizen. His frame that once stood erect before the thunders of British artillery, was bending over the staff of infirmity; but see him aroused and animated upon some great national question in which his feelings were enlisted, and you could see in his eyes a hundred battle-fields, and every one a victory—you could catch the inspiration of the fire that burned in his manly bosom when in the field giving command to an eager and patriotic soldiery. Of him it might be said in truth,

"The elements
So mix'd in him, that Nature might stand up
And say to all the world—this is a man."

When I took my leave of him for the last time, with the tenderness of a father he took me by the hand, and with tears streaming down his faded cheek, he invoked Heaven's choicest, purest blessings upon my head along the rough journey of life. Never shall I forget that last interview. I'll retain it in this heart of hearts as long as I live. I'll remember his council, and practice upon the principles he has laid down. He knew he was not mistaken, when he said that by the aid of an untarnished moral character, and unremitting industry, a youth, poor and without influential friends as he may be, can be successful in all his laudable enterprises. Upon this, let every young man build his hopes, who wishes eventually to record his name high on the temple of fame, and en- roll it eventually with those of the Washingtons, the Franklins, the Jeffersons and Jacksons who have gone before him. Though the waves of misfortune may dash furiously about him, and the clouds of opposition arise upon the horizon of his hopes, let him not be discour- aged, for Jackson too had all these to overcome. But the more numerous and imminent the perilous scenes through which he had so pass, the brighter is the crown of glory that he wore. We may talk in extravagant praises of the host of worthies whose services have been employed without wariness in advancing our country, but where is a name that adorns the pages of our histo- ry with a brighter halo around it, save the Father of his Country? True it is, some have their fears about the probable degeneracy of statesman virtues, but let them not despair. We may not point to a few public men,

and say of them it is true that there stand the choicest
spirits of the age, &c.

[Mr. Allen seems not to have finished the writing out of this
Speech.]

REMARKS OF MR. ALLEN.

*On the 8th of January, 1846, on the Bill proposing to erect
a Statue and Monument to Gen. Jackson.*

Mr. Speaker:—When the proposition was first made
to erect a statue of "imperishable bronze," to be placed
in the Capitol of the State when finished, and a monument in accordance with the recommendation of the Gov-
eruor in his Inaugural Address, to be placed on the bank
of the "noblest river in the world, where the millions
who will pass for ages and ages to come, may pause and
gaze upon it with wonder and admiration," in perpetuation of the memory of Gen. Andrew Jackson, I did not
intend to say one word upon the subject. I do not *now*
rise for the purpose of discussing the merits of the bill,
nor to pronounce a studied and inflated panegyric upon
the life and character of Gen. Jackson. He needs none
at my hands. The country he contributed so largely
and freely to defend is vocal with his praise. His public acts from the time he entered the councils of the nation (to say nothing of his military prowess,) to the day
he retired with dignity to the shades of private life, are
sufficient and enduring testimonials of his greatness.—
These have been portrayed to us in the most eloquent
language by the gentlemen from the county of Sumner,
(Mr. Guild,) who enjoys the honor of introducing the bill,
and by the rich oratory of the Representative from
Washington, (Mr. Haynes.) They have expressed the

hope which I here take occasion to renew, that the bill will pass by acclamation—that however widely and materially certain members may differ with Gen. Jackson upon political questions, they will illustrate their magnanimity by awarding to his memory its just deserts.— That a portion of his political enemies in this body will do this, we have the most convincing and satisfactory testimony.

It is a cherished desire by members on this side of the House that nothing of a party character shall enter into our deliberations upon this question. Such a feeling and disposition on such an occasion, should animate every bosom. It is a state of things most "devoutly to be wished." These expectations and hopes may yet be realized. No person would rejoice at it with more unfeigned satisfaction than myself. Who wishes to see the glorious 8th of January dessecrated by the representatives of the people, in widening the breach between the two parties, when an identity of interest should make them more united? If there be such an individual, I can only say that I do not envy his feelings. After premising these remarks, it is due to candor and truth, that I should say, from the indications made, we will not act together with that unanimity and concert so ardently hoped for. Already has the demon of party been aroused from its lair. Its tendency is to frighten members from the support of such measures as they conscientiously approve. To those who are aiding in fanning the flames, I would say with becoming respect, beware unless you suffer by the conflagration you are instrumental in creating. Those few choice sprits whose political identities are adverse to my own, who have the independence and moral firmness to sustain the bill, will be greeted and cheered by the plau-

dits of the liberal men of all parties. But with the
course honorable gentlemen may think proper to pursue
upon this question, I have nothing to do. They, like
myself, are responsible to their country for their acts.

I will not, however, disguise the fact, that I was not
a little surprised at the introduction of the amendment
to the bill by the Representive from the country of Madison (Mr. Bullock.) Knowing that there was an inkling
towards opposition to the bill as it was first introduced
on the part of some of our whig friends, and in order
that they might be reconciled to vote for it, by general
consent, we agreed to strike out the two first sections of
the bill which made an appropriation from the Treasury.
After doing this, we had the assurance that they would
cease their hostility to the measure. But, sir, we were
mistaken. It pains me to make this announcement, but
it is *true*. What now do we hear? A voice of opposition coming up by way of amendment, after previous
concessions and compromises. And by whom has it ori-
ginated? By a leading member of the whig party, as
personated in the Representative from Madison (Mr. Bullock.) The amendment, to say the least of it, is an insidious attack upon the bill. This may be strong language, but not stronger than the occasion will justify.
The gentleman may be sincere when he expresses a hope
that the bill will pass. I don't stand up here to impeach
his sincerity. But, sir, we will try men's faith by their
works. Here is a Procrustean standard by which the
member may regulate his friendship for the bill. It may
be found in the proposition made by the gentleman from
Washington (Mr. Haynes.) I now call upon my friend
from Madison, for whom I cherish none other than the
kindest feelings, to unite with us upon this question.

What is the object of the amendment offered by the gentleman from Madison? It proposes also the erection of a statue to the memory of George Washington, "the defender of his country, the founder of liberty, the friend of man." To the amendment, if it had been offered as a substantive proposition, and in good faith, no individual could reasonably object. Every Tennessean, *especially*, who is proud of his "own, his native land," would be glad to see such a statue to the memory of the greatest man that ever lived, who "in the annals of modern greatness, stands alone, and the noblest names of antiquity lose their lustre in his presence." But serious fears are entertained that it will have a tendency to embarrass the passage of the bill. If satisfied that such will not be the case, I would gladly see it incorporated as a part of the bill. So far, however, as the perpetuation of his fame is concerned, no monument need be erected. He has built his "monument in the hearts of his countrymen," and his fame is co-extensive with civilization itself. But it has been an immemorial and time-hallowed custom to erect such monuments to the distinguished dead in all ages of the world. The United States is no less proud of her great men than other nations. *She will ever embalm, in greatful recollection, the invincible defenders of her liberty.

> "Patriots have toiled, and in their country's cause
> Bled nobly. And their deeds as they deserve,
> Receive proud recompense. We give in charge,
> Their names to the sweet lyre. The historic muse,
> Proud of her treasure, marches with it down
> To latest times; and sculpture in her turn
> Gives bond, in stone, and ever-during brass,
> To guard them, and immortalize her trust."

The erection of a statue to the father of his country would seem to be more appropriately a national object which every citizen of the Union, however humble and obscure, may contribute his free-will offering. In the Capitol at Washington stands in unmutilated and unsullied grandeur his sculptured form. It belongs to the whole nation. If gentlemen are sincere in what they profess, and I impeach the purity of no man's motives, the time may not be far remote when the Capitol of our own proud and chivalrous State will be ornamented and adorned with living, speaking and eloquent statutes of Washington and Jackson. As their names are to be linked together in connection with whatever is virtuous, chivalrous and great in the history of the country they fought to sustain, it may not be inappropriate that a statue be erected to each, and placed side by side in the Capitol of the State. Like Washington, Jackson needs no monument, so far as the perpetuation of the memory of his great deeds are concerned. As long as the 8th of January is remembered, he will be heralded as the greatest captain of the age in which he lived. While the great father of waters continues to roll by the monument to be planted on its bank, bearing upon its ample and majestic bosom the wealth of the surrounding country, it will murmur his deathless praise. To use the language of another "his fame is eternity, and residence creation." Being "first in war, first in peace and first in the hearts of his countrymen," he was second to none in the social relations of private life. But I shall not dwell upon those virtues so admirably illustrated in his character. I wish to see erected on yonder hill a magnificent edifice—one that will be highly creditable to the State we represent. When completed, I am willing to see the statuary forms of Washington and Jackson within it, as guardian angels to preside over the deliberations of future Legislatures for all time to come. And when the madness of party shall disturb the harmony so essential to the administration of wholesome laws, by these images they may be reminded of their councils while living. Let them read the prophetic language that is addressed to them, to avoid against the baleful effects of party spirit. Among the ancients it was a saying that

"While stands the Coliseum, Rome shall stand."

Let this kind of feeling animate our people, and nerve their arms to action. Let them resolve that as long as that edifice shall endure, *aye*, as long as the hill upon which it rests shall remain, our country with her free institutions, shall stand, as the proudest monument of human wisdom. And let them constantly bear in mind that those inestimable privileges which they enjoy under the auspices of such institutions, have been transmitted of them unimpaired through the instrumentality of Washington and Jackson.

Transatlantic nations may speak in terms derogatory to our people and government—they may attempt a depreciation of the merits of our great men, but when an impartial verdict shall be rendered, as it WILL be, it will appear that for all the elements of true greatness there are Americans who can honorably compare with those of any other country. In saying this I am not ignorant of the impression that prevails, that it is impossible for the United States to produce, in the strict sense of the term, genuine statesmen—that her politicians are numerous, her statesmen none—that we cannot point to them in the exultation of our hearts and exclaim, "here stand the choicest spirits of their age; the greatest wits, the noblest orators, the wisest politicians, the most illustrious patriots. Here they stand, whose hands have been raised for their country, whose magical eloquence has shook the spheres, whose genius has poured out strains worthy the inspiration of the gods, whose lives were devoted to the purity of their principles, whose memories were bequeathed to a race greatful for benefits received from their sufferings and their sacrifices." Such an insinuation is as illiberal as it is untrue. However invidious may be the fault-finders and hypocritical writers of the old world, they are constrained to award to Gen. Jackson a high niche in the temple of renown. With the gentleman from Sumner, (Mr. Guild,) it may be said that he has emphatically "filled the measure of his country's glory," and his name will *never* die.

> "Rear strong the vast memorial high,
> That Freedom's future sons may come to bless
> His memory, and breathe new spirits there,
> And at that altar-shrine, like mighty sons
> Of Hannibal of old, most proudly swear
> Like him to fight, like him to nobly die.
> The deathless *foes* of fading tyranny—
> That down from age to age the truth may live,
> *Republics not ungreatful are*, and wreaths can weave
> And monuments upraise for patriots true,
> Arising, like their deeds, from common dust,
> O'er common men, and pointing to the skies,
> To note that, *as the stars*, they glitter there!"

His deeds of matchless daring, and his inflexible devotion to his country, stand like a tower pointing magnificently to Heaven, exciting the envy and admiration of the world. His faults, which no man can claim exemption, it is hoped, have descended with him to the oblivion of the tomb. Peace be to his manes! is the patriot's prayer.

His resplendent virtues, and he had many, should be emblazoned upon the pages of history, and left as a rich heritage to the millions of freemen who are to succeed him in all time to come. As the patriot, the soldier and sage, full of years and full of honors, has gone down to his grave in peace with the world and his God, let his virtues be resurrected—let them continue to live in the song of the poet and eulogium of the orator. Let ingenuous youths, as they assemble together around one national altar on the annual return of the jubilee of the 8th of January, herald forth his admirable traits of character. They will never cease to emulate those Socratic virtues of which he was the representative—that they will never forget the obligations they are under to promote the cherished interests of their country and advance the "symbols of her triumph"—and that no consideration of personal aggrandizement will ever be the cause of an abandonment of those great and important principles for which he fought, is confidently and ardently hoped. If there be any thing on earth calculated to disturb the patriot's repose, and cause his great spirit to rise up and condemn it, it is a base and treacherous attempt to sever this glorious Union. *Never, never,* may our people be so blind and insensible to their interests and the happiness of those who are to succeed them, as to consent to have it "rent asunder!" If our government is ever to be free, prosperous and happy—if the sun of her greatness is not to set in the starless night of despotism—if our brightest hopes and anticipations are to be realized in reference to the continued security and welfare of our country, our people must be *virtuous, en lightened and brave.* They should adopt the favorite maxim to "ask nothing that is not right, and submit to nothing that is wrong." They should watch with distrust that public servant or diplomatic functionary who would consent to an abandonment of one inch of our territory where our title is "clear and unquestionable." With such a determination our country is secure. *"Esto perpetua,"* is written in characters of light upon her destiny. When the monuments of her glory shall have fallen to decay, her peerless form will still stand up like a giantess full of proportion, animated with life, and buoyant with anticipations. But I shall not pause to weave visions about the future in reference to the perpetuity of our institutions. May the memory of his deeds who has reflected a radiance of glory around Tennessee and the Union, be eternal! May every youth, like the young Carthagenian, swear upon the altar of his country never to forsake her, and with the defender of the emporium of the west, at all events and under every circumstance, "Our Federal Union, it *must* be preserved."

A SPEECH ON TEMPERANCE, DELIVERED IN 1844, IN LAWRENCEBURG.

Ladies and Gentlemen:—It has been but a week, since I had an opportunity of addressing you upon the subject of Temperance. It gives me much pleasure, upon this occasion, to assure you that my opinions in regard to Temperance associations, and the amount of good resulting from them, have not altered or changed in the least. The same burning zeal which you have manifested in this cause, is cherished not only in other parts of our State, but throughout the whole Union. I have witnessed the exhibitions of this spirit in every place where it has been my fortune to visit. People are beginning to see the imminency of the peril to which they are exposed, and are devising means by which the fatal blow may be warded off. They have ascertained that nothing is more invulnerable to the darts which temptation is continually assailing us with, than the impenetrable shield which the Temperance pledge throws around us. With this bulwark around us we can stand secure, and bid defiance to the foul monster. The Temperance Societies have been productive of much good—that they have broken the galling chains under which weeping humanity has been afflicted—that the morals of the people are much improved—that religion, "pure, unpensioned and unstipendary," as it should be, fiuds an easier access to the human heart—that individual and national prosperity is advanced by their potent agency and magical influence, no man in his common senses will pretend to contradict or deny. The fact stares us too boldly in the face for a negation to be raised. One thing is equally flagrant and undeniable—that if it does no good, the Temperance Society does no harm or injury. If we look at it in this light, and we can view it in no other, we cannot consistently and conscientiously, I am persuaded, raise an objection against it, though we may not aid in supporting it. If we do not intend to be sober, reflecting men ourselves, we certainly will not envy the same in others, when it is in our power to do likewise. If our friend in almost hopeless misery, upon the troubled waves of life's tempestuous ocean, siezes upon a plank or floating mass, by which he can pass securely over the lashing and surging billows to the long sought haven of rest, will we, though determined to sink by the leaden weights of our own cares, snatch from the resistless grasp of that friend the only hope that flits across his bewildered mind? If we set a resolution not to join the Temperance Society, let us use no exertions to prevent others doing it.

I design, gentlemen, to be very plain in the few re-marks which I shall submit for your consideration, and shall by no means be personal in my casual allusions.—I should be very much mortified to think I had wounded the feelings of any one of my respected audience, by a reference to such examples necessary, in the course of my speech. I believe many have been kept from joining us on account of the unmerited abuse we have been in the habit of heaping upon the intemperate. We should use milder means towards them, and address ourselves to their reason—to their judgment. I may use pretty strong language myself before I am done, but you will please remember that it is the crime and not the man I inveigh. The man I respect and admire, but the crime I loathe and hate. Although Temperance Societies have effected much to man's social enjoyment, much more still remains to be done. Intemperance still stalks with a broad front in our midst. Distilleries are still sending forth the poisonous liquid. It infects the atmosphere around its vicinity, and brings superlative misery and wo upon its attendants or visitors. Our Legislature would have reflected credit upon itself if it had stoped this evil at its fountain head, and stopped up all the ave-nues through which it is entailed upon the people. A still-house is unquestionably one of the greatest curses thas ever befel a community. The first one that ever was erected, was in the flames of hell, and the Devil himself was the chief architect—he laid the corner-stone with his impious hands. In him the materials are fitly framed together, and groweth to an unholy temple in his Satanic Majesty. His strong-holds must first be broken up before we can expect harmony and order pervading our country. But there is another wall behind which he has entrenched himself. That wall must also be demolished. Groceries must step retailing the malady.— It must be considered disreputable to engage in such business. I heard an individual say that a grocery-keeper was keeping a toll-gate on the turnpike to hell — Public opinion is not yet right upon this subject. It should frown down any attempts to establish such doggeries, and if the country is to be entirely purged of drunkards, *it* must do the work. It is the tribunal to which all appeals must be taken.

It is not my purpose, on the present occasion, to speak of the deleterious effects of ardent spirits upon the physical powers of man, nor do I intend to make a nomenclature of diseases, and hold it up before you. You have doubtless been enlightened upon this subject by men better calculated to do it justice than myself. Every candid, thinking mind unhesitatingly accedes that the effects upon the system are deplorable. This being too plain and manifest to occasion the shadow of a doubt to arise, I shall proceed in my simple manner to notice some of the many objections which are daily urged against our Temperance Societies. There is a respectable class of citizens amongst us who say they are strong and decided temperance men, but contend that we carry the joke entirely too far. They believe in Temperance, but can't stand this thing of tetotalism.— Temperance Societies, as they were first instituted, answered a very good purpose at that time; but will not suit the present crisis. Those societies merely opened the way for the millenial dawn of total abstinence. Thus it was with the colonists when they claimed all the rights and immunities of British subjects, but when independence was in their grasp, they declared themselves. "free, sovereign and independent people." That's the declaration we wish to make, and we earnestly entreat you to lend your aid and influence in entirely throwing off the galling chains which bind us in worse than British vassalage. If we were not to pursue this plan, and tolerate temperate or moderate drinking, where would we place the line of demarkation between a temperate man and a drunkard? The individual himself must be the judge, and if he gets dead drunk, he can say that he has only taken it in moderation. You see then, this doctrin won't answer the purpose.

And just here I make the bold and emphatic declaration, that every individual who drinks ardent spirits, either in moderation or otherwise, is in the strict sense, a bona fide drunkard. This is as plain a proposition as that things which are equal to the same thing, are equal to each other. Now for the proof. How much of the article, let me ask, will it take to make you drunk? Do you say a quart? Well. Won't a pint do it? You say no. Well, but if the first pint won't make you drunk, you have acknowledged that the second one will. Well, which one of these pints has had the greater agency in making you drunk? That is what you don't know.— Here then is the unvarnished fact. If a quart will make a man drunk, a pint will make him half drunk, half pint a fourth drunk, a gill an eighth, and so on. Thus we see he is a drunkard, let him take as little as he pleases. This is no syllogism, for every drop of the spirits must have its effect, otherwise you might take a barrel and you would feel no sensations of a toper.

Some individuals contend that the Temperance Society is useless—that if one can quit drinking after having joined it, he can quit without joining it. And how is he to do it, but by setting a determination tacitly, that he will ever after disuse ardent spirits? Don't we know how susceptible we are of yielding to temptations, in spite of all our determinations and resolves? We all make the most earnest vows and sacred promises, by the tacit consent of our unbridled passions and unhallowed inclinations, but break them with perfect indifference.—Its our nature to do so. The experience of every one who hears me, bears ample, unqualified testimony to this fact. We see then, that this objection is futile, and founded only for the purpose of occasional dissipation. Here, I trust, is another successful refutation of the many objections to temperance societies.

There is another class of individuals who contend that the Church is a sufficient Temperance Society. Well, sure enough it is, but do they who profess to belong to the church, abstain from all uses of ardent spirits? Of late it seems there are as many members of the church getting drunk, as any other sort. It is with unfeigned regret that I say it, but truth must be proclaimed from every house-top. Besides this, there are a majority of people who belong to no church, and I suppose from such objections, that they can get drunk with impunity. There are no such weighty responsibilities resting upon them, which an initiation into religious orders impose, and as a matter of course owe no duty at all to society, in any of its ramifications. If you will believe me, Mr. President, I would rather undertake to convert ten rank infidels to the doctrines of christianity, than one of these long-faced, sanctimonious, orthodox nominal christians, who goes about with the Bible under his arms, and quotes from it in support of his side, to be a warm, thorough-going temperance advocate. There would be more probability of my succeeding. I have but little confidence in such christians. Their prospects for heaven, in my humble opinion, hang upon uncertainties. The Bible authorises no man to get-drunk.—— It gives an admonitory lesson to all who indulge in drinking. "Who hath wo? Who hath sorrow? Who hath contentions? Who hath babbling? Who hath wounds without cause? Who hath redness of eyes?—— They that tarry long at the wine; they that seek mixed wine. Look not thou upon the wine when it is red, when it giveth its color in the cup, when it moveth itself aright. At the last it biteth like a serpent and stingeth like an adder." Some dreadful apprehensions and fearful omens have been awakened in this matter by those who profess to divine future events, especially in regard to the tendency of the system which we propose to your consideration, and which they oppose. They do not, I am apprehensive, entertain very serious fears upon this subject, for we have had no example of like nature in the history of the world. And what is it, after all?—— Why they say, take care, you are upon dangerous premises—you are about to unite Church and State.—— Strange anomaly indeed! Is it the Church of England you are alarmed at? We see christians of all denominations meeting in good feeling upon this broad platform. The embittered animosity that may be existing between them in regard to religious dogmas and creeds, entirely disappears. Upon this subject they meet and embrace each other. They are all one in this cause. Why the Whigs and Democrats, as much as they hate each other, are all friends when the banner of Temperance is placed before them. Are there then any exclusive pretensions in this matter? There are none. The Temperance opposition can find no subterfuge upon this point. Their arguments are their own refutation. But there is another very serious objection which con- stitutes the most plausible pretext for hostility to our cause that has yet been considered. I allude to those gentlemen who are so chary of their inalienable and im- prescriptible rights. Who appear to disdain oppression in any of its protean forms. Who would not wantonly stain with their sacred hands, our country's bright es- cutcheon, and whose zeal for her promotion burns with untold enthusiasm. What! shall an American citizen baselessly and ingloriously sign away his liberties for which his progenitors so nobly bled--so nobly died?-- Let us not imprecate the memory of the immortal dead. whose deeds and enterprises illumine the annals of our country. Let us not dim the bright lustre of their char- acters, by imputing to them things so disreputable--so unworthy. If the invaluable immunity and transcend- ant liberty of getting gloriously drunk--if the liberty of abusing your family and children, unconscientiously--if the liberty of laying in the gutters with your four-footed brethren, exposed to the pitiless storms--if the liberty of having black eyes and bloody noses--of weak minds and debilitated frames be the legacy transmitted to you by your forefathers, better, far better had they never broken the chains of European thraldom, and handed down to you unimpaired this boasted though much abused privilege. We have many privileges which we

dare not exercise. What would you think of a man of
such invidiousness that he would cut off his nose to spite
his face? And he has unquestionably the right to do it.
Is it the part of wisdom to exercise such dangerous privileges? The rats had undoubtedly the undeniable
right to hell the cat, but when they considered the peril
in doing it, they abandoned the idea. The discharge of
such a function is fraught, not unfrequently, with the
most direful calamities. When the serpent has prepared
to bury its fangs into your person, is it depriving you of
a very precious liberty, either to bruise its head or force
you from it, thereby preventing your receiving the ma-
lignant poison of death? Such is the privation you
would be likely to endure were you to join the Temperance Society. We don't want you inconsiderately and
thoughtlessly to deprive yourself of any of the rights
and immunities of freemen. Do we propose to do it?--
Reason tells you no. Outraged and provoked human
nature tells you no. The cries and wailings of the oppressed and unfortunate, in tones louder than thunder,
tell you no. The voice of poverty, and the lamentations of the disconsolate tell you no. It is upon this
principle that Satan acts. He says through the inspired
pen of the poet,

> "To rule is worth ambition though in Hell;
> Better to reign in Hell than serve in Heaven."

Whilst there are many among us who heartily approve of our associations of this kind, we find many in
that category who refuse to join the Society. Some of
them too, are abstemious, considerate, sober men. And
what's their objection? Simply that it would be doing
no good--that they have no influence with others.--

Well, you may say it, but I should dislike very much to tell either of you that you have no influence in the world. If I were to address myself thus to a man, I should expect him to maul me with his fist, or uncase a howie-knife for my benefit. If to a lady, I should expect her to tell me immediately, without a moment's reflection, that she has as much influence as I have; or its equivolent. Show me an individual that has no influence in the world, and I do sincerely pity him. His God would not deign to receive him, and the Devil would not own him. I have too high an opinion of human nature to believe any man is so lost to all the attributes and qualities of a man, as to declare, conscientiously, that he has no influence over some boon companion or relative. I can never persuade myself it is true. Then you are obligated to join with us, in order to induce others on the broad highway to do likewise. If you have a friend or relative who is inclined to habits of dissipation, you are bound by the strongest ties of affection, to use your influence to reclaim that friend or relative from the snares into which he is rapidly hastening. If a friend of ours were placed in an upper story of a large edifice, and the report was given that the building was on fire, and there were no possibility of escape but by leaping from a window, we would assemble around the place, fix an easy place for him to light upon, with outstretched arms, and at the top of our voices, we would entreat him, exhort him, encourage him, to sum up resolution and save himself, before he is enveloped in the broad sheet of fire raging frightfully and terrifically beneath or around him. This would seem to be the natural impulse of our feelings, before time would allow us to reflect upon the most expeditious mode of rescuing or delivering our friend. But here is a case in which all the current flow of feeling and sensibility seems to be stopped up by cold and careless indifference. And it is one in which greater things are periled—greater, infinitely greater interests are involved. He is not only placed in an eminently dangerous situation in regard to security and protection from injury, but the fires of hell are enkindled within his very vitals, which are not only extinguishing life, but destroying the immortal soul. This is done, unfortunately, though unpiteously by his own suicidal hands. He is the author of his own guilt and crime. Does it not comport with the character of a good citizen, nay, is it not his bounden duty to use his best endeavors to reform that man—to wrest from his grasp the deadly weapons of his own destruction—to extinguish those raging fires which are insiduously and indubitably effecting his eternal ruin? It is lamentably true, that we will see the brightest ornaments of creation cloven down and obscured by the consideration of our own personal gratification. Some would see the best interests of society destroyed, and the brightest hopes of glory dimmed, before they would discommode themselves in a small degree, by abandoning the intoxicating cup. If it were not counteracting the laws of Nature, it does seem to me ardent spirits would never be used. If it were produced in abundance by Nature—if the brooks and rills in their course would murmur whiskey—if old ocean in her awful grandeur were whiskey—if the clouds above us were to distil in showers nothing but unadulterated, genuine, bald-face whiskey, what a world would we have after a while? What a band of jolly fellows we would have? What inhuman crimes would not be perpetrated? We would be like so many tigers eagerly watching for our prey. One tiger would come up to his brother tiger, and enjoy themselves by howling, and growling, and fighting. All creation would resound with the intoxicating animals. The earth upon which we tread would deviate from its orbit, and imitate the motions of a drunken man. The sea would disgorge itself of its mighty inhabitants, producing a stench that would taint the atmosphere by putrifying carcasses. Nature never designed a man should drink any thing that destroys his [equilibrium. This earth was never intended to be inhabited by an order of beings who deprive themselves of their reason, by indulgence in dissipation. If a man drink regularly, though perhaps in strict moderation, in nine cases out of ten, he will eventually become a drunkard. It is without question the most dangerous way he can indulge. Much better if he would drink irregularly and to a greater extent at the time. If one dram is taken, another must be taken also to keep it company, and such repetitions are continued until the individual is "seas over." One crime opens the way to another. "What harm is there in a pipe," says one friend to another, to which his companion replied, "none that I know, except smoking induces drinking—drinking induces intoxication—intoxication induces bile—bile induces dispepsia—dispepsia induces pulmonary consumption—pulmonary consumption induces death—put that in your pipe and smoke it." Now I say nothing derogatory to the practice of smoking, but merely intend to declare that one error is a stepping block to another. It is useless for men to talk of their power to command themselves, and not transcend the boundaries of moderation. I heard an individual not long since, give a narrative of his life upon this subject, and although it was a little metphysical, it contained a good moral. He said, amid the allurements and fascinations of pleasure, with the gales of unclouded prosperity visiting him, when age, with none of its appurtenances, knew him, he concluded to take a voyage upon life's ruffled waves. With many of his youthful companions, he stepped on board the ship Indulgence, freighted with Misery, and bound for the city of Destruction. It was his purpose to go only to the port of Moderation, which was but a short way off. The sails were hoisted, the news "all's well" was heard, and the way they went. Every thing appeared as tranquil as the unruffled surface of the silver lake.— No demon raised its black and terrific form before him. The smiles of Heaven played disportingly around the gallant vessel. His eyes became fastened upon objects on the way, and his ears were saluted by the syren song of pleasure. He never looks to calculate the distance he has passed; nor does he keep a look-out for the place of his destination. Directly he is informed by some kind and affectionate friend that he has long since passed it by. He is surprised at the intelligence, but promises most faithfully to stop a short distance below, at a place called "Just Enough." Unconscious of the accelerated velocity he has acquired, he passes that in the rear also. He passes a little farther*down the stream of life, and comes to a little village called Hiccough town, but he stops not there. Still onward is his course. The waves of trouble begin to dash furiously against his once peaceful mind. Their undulations, however, did not sufficiently alarm him. In a few brief moments he finds himself at Puke City, whose streets are filth and mud.— He tarries here but a short time, visiting only the most prominent parts—such as Red-nose, and Red-eye street,

and Skin-shin alley—to say nothing of Empty-purse
lane, and the bye ways to Poverty, which are innumerable. But few more sands of the hour are exhausted till
he finds himself at Drunkard's Island. The City of Destruction is in sight—he pauses to think, the waves bearing him rapidly to its harbor. He begins to look around
him and to view his position. The most of his companions with whom he set out on life's morning march have
perished. He is led to ask himself the question, "What
shall I do to be saved." He raises his eyes and beholds the City of Refuge a short distance off, whose
walls are massy gold—whose streets sparkle with dia-
monds—whose temples are dedicated to wisdom. Upon
the loftiest summit thereabouts are seen its peaceful inhabitants—the members of the Temperance reformation
—with their arms extended, their voices tuned to their
highest note. They warn him of his danger, and exhort him to fly to them for safety. Although he was
becoming callous and indifferent, by their importunate
entreaties he leaps over-board the evil bound vessel—
takes a "cold-water" shoot, and is felicitously, fortu-
nately reclaimed. If there be one unfortunate individual who has visited these places, I will admonish him
to stop! for grim death is before him. As one disinterested, I would invite him, by a regard for his standing
and well-being, to touch not—taste not—handle not.—
If the serpent once entwines its hiddeous folds around
you, you are gone forever. The fate of Larcoon will
be stamped upon your destiny. I have read the fable
of Circe who was celebrated for her art in magic, and
whoever drank of her cup was immediately transformed
into swine. We have a poison in our midst, which men
deliberately, and I might say fearlessly take, which not

M

only transforms them into beasts, but at the same time deprives them of their reason. Is there no Ulysses to release you, or Physician Hermes to administer to your relief? The Temperance Society is the only salutary remedy. By submitting to its requisitions you are restored to your reason, and rescued from the den of infamy and vice. Who is there in this free land of America, who can calmly look at the history of the past, and more especially of individual man, and not feel a sense of responsibility resting upon him, to remedy, as far as he is able, the malady which is striking a fatal blow at the happiness and perpetuity of governments, and blasting all the bright and glowing anticipations of gifted intelligence? Read the battle of Hastings at which the English were drunk when the Normans headed by William, the conqueror, gained a decided victory, and learn a moral from it.—— Look to the degradation and hopelessness that have been entailed upon individuals, as it were, by the seducing enchantments of wine. See the ingenuous youths upon whose characters and reputations are engrafted stains which all the waters of Lethe, nor ocean can wash out, and say you are not under obligations to aid in banishing this evil. Patriotism and humanity revolt at such listless dormency. Does any man ask for an evidence of the utility of such a system as the one which we have proposed to your consideration? Can he see the good it has done and is still doing, and then ask for additional testimony? If the whole host of reformed drunkards could be marshaled together in solid column, and be permitted to speak at once upon this subject, their simultaneous voices would be heard above the hoarse muttering thunder, telling in undying accents, the obligations they owe to the Temperance Society. And could the affectionate wives and daughters of the land, whose husbands and fathers have been rescued from the curse of this damning evil be heard, their voices would doubtless go up to heaven sweeter than the music of David's harp upon the troubled bosom of Israel's king, and there seal the declaration that Temperance Societies are invaluable. The angel smile that plays innocently upon the glowing cheek—the heaven-descending rays of prosperity upon the frugal—and the thanks-givings of the pure in heart, which are embalmed in eternal remembrance—all bear conclusive and satisfactory evidence of their utility. Who have a better right to speak in this matter than the ladies? Not that they have ever disgraced themselves by intemperance, but because they have had to endure the vituperations and abuses of which intemperate husbands are generally so unsparing. No wonder then, that they have such anxieties in this matter. No wonder they have nearly all come quietly into the fold, and are endeavoring to bring after them the other sex. They know full well that they have children to raise and train up for usefulness and honor, and that unless they are taught the lessons of sobriety in youth, the fruits of old age will be misery and crime. Go on then, ladies, I beseech you, in this glorious cause. Unfold with your own hands that broad banner which is the sheet-anchor of our independence. May heaven smile upon your efforts, and may heaven be your reward. And now, in conclusion, let me exhort you, gentlemen, by the sacred obligations which are resting on you—by a regard for your own eternal happiness—by a debt which you owe to your country and your God, suspend your course in dissipation and be men, and christian men. This would be my advice to you, though it was the last

word I had to say. I can have no design in the world
to deceive you. I am prompted by disinterestedness
entirely in addressing you. May you not feel yourselves
disinterested in your actions upon this subject in regard
to your own welfare. Make up your determination
speedily, and act according to the dictates of your dis-
passionate judgments. Remember that delays are often
dangerous. When Capua was taken, the walls of Carthage trembled. The way to do is to "try all things,
and hold fast that which is good." The influence of
example is great and salutary. Enlist yourselves among
us, and let us continue to battle against the foe to human happiness. Our rulers are beginning to help us,
and we may receive encouragement from it. I observed in some of the newspaper prints, a few days since,
that the Legislature of New York, at its last sitting,
formed a Temperance Society for the benefit of its own
members. If our own State Legislature would only imitate their example, I have no doubt but they would
have shorter sessions, and pass *better* laws for the people.

AN ESSAY ON THE MIND.

A great deal has been said and written about the mind;
its faculties and developments: but it has not been ascertained, as far as our information will permit us to
judge, at what period its mightiest energies mature.—
From the fact of some intellects developing sooner than
others, we would infer that this question never will be
settled definitely. Some minds expand to the fullest limits in youth, whilst others, under the same kind of culture, are not equally vigorous at a more advanced age.
Why this is the case, men of intelligence have not yet

agreed. It is generally conceded, however, that between the age of twenty-five and thirty, (the precise time not being stated) the mind will be as stong as it will be ever after, and a period beyond this might be fixed upon with a degree of certainty. There have been precocious geniuses in the world who attracted considerable notoriety, and gained merited applause on account of the attainments they had made long before they had laid aside the toga of puberty. The Muses were gladdened at the effusions of Pollock and Kirk White, who seemed to have been destined by nature to enjoy an enviable pre-eminence among the literary characters of the world, but their sun went down while it was yet day. Early death seems to be the fate of those who make a brilliant display upon the theatre of life while very young. It is a remarkable fact, that those early geniuses whose productions have been preserved, and of whose characters history gives an account, and who have lived to an old age, seldom ever surpass their first efforts. This may not be universally true, but it is confirmed in many characters of whose writings we are familiar. That Pollock, had he lived until he was three-score years and ten, would never have given to the world a work superior to the "Course of Time," I believe is the opinion of a great many. In consideration of the many examples of like nature, of which our own history abounds, it does seem evident that in most cases, that premature geniuses are subject unavoidably to premature decay. Destiny must accomplish its work. The budding intellect is often nipped as it were in the bloom. It decays, droops, and dies in the dawning of spring. It is said that genius is celebrated for its peculiarity and excentricity.—— We find some strange features in the character of every man of superior ability. It was said of Molanus that, under the influence of a mental hallucination, he was unwilling to go along the streets for fear he would be picked up by a fowl and swallowed for a barley. These are some of the symptoms of genius. It should be a matter of great concern, that the mind should be directed to its proper and legitimate goal. It appears to be true, that a wrong direction has been given to the laudable efforts of the struggling intellect. The first inquiry in relation to this matter should be, in what is the individual most likely to succeed? This being ascertained satisfactorily, all others should be laid aside. I am not one of those agreeing with Quintellian that the same faculty of mind which made Germanicus an accomplished general, would, with the requisit amount of attention and care, have made him an excellent poet or orator. It is not denied but that some minds could succeed admirably in almost any department, but it is not believed that he cannot master one thing better, more expeditiously, and with greater facility than some other. In a word, every man has what is called a genius for a particular thing. What we mean to assert is, that Addison had more talent for writing than he had for speaking—that the Duke of Wellington is better qualified for the camp than the Queen's parlor or the House of Commons.— This assertion if true, puts at naught the idea advanced that the mind is originally a perfect blank—for if we reason from this data we would conclude that with the same perseverance in the influence of like circumstances every man would be equally intelligent, which cannot possibly be true. It may be that our intellect is too short to penetrate the obscurity that lingers around this subject, but by a parity of reasoning we draw different conclusions. To believe the American Savage, with the same tuition, could have penetrated the dark recesses of science like a Newton, and opened a new field of discovery and speculation, is to admit things which experience and history teach is untrue. Around some species of the human race nature has erected an impenetrable wall. Their intellectual visions are as short and indistinct as the mole that forces its way through the earth. Were they to live a full century, surrounded by all desirable means of improvement, it is not probable they would ever make any important advancements in literary attainments. Where is the excellent schollar—the correct writer—and popular orator among the Africans? When a thousand years, pregnant with advantages and encouragements, shall have passed over them, it will be found that they have not made one single step in the march of mind. One defect is, they don't seem to have the will—the ambition, and zeal to urge them to action. They are too much subject to the influences of the grosser passions of our nature. The constant direction of their efforts is downward and not upward. They would rather burrow in the earth than soar heavenward on fancy's eagle pinions.

Men may speculate at pleasure upon the wisdom which Providence displays in all his works, but one thing forces itself upon us irresistibly: that a portion of the human family are destined, eternally, to live in a starless night of unproductive ignorance, because they possess faculties insusceptible of the smallest degree of improvement. If this be true, and it bears the seal of plausibility upon its front, it would seem at first blush, that iron-handed fatalism had fastened its grasp firmly and steadfastly upon the destiny of those who claim to be endowed, in some degree, with a moity of that rationality which characterises intellectual intelligences from those destitute of mind. But there are things which bear the semblance of truth, which are flagrant falsehoods. The designs of the Deity may be impugned, like those of man, without any just reason or complaint. It is enough for man to know, that his duty requires him to make all the improvement of which he is able, whatever be the restraints and incumbrances, and then he will have discharged his whole duty to himself and his Creator.

AN ESSAY ON THE COMPARATIVE HAPPINESS OF INTELLIGENT AND BARBAROUS NATIONS.

Much has been written and said about the comparative happiness of civilized and barbarous nations, but so far from settling the dispute upon this subject, it is involved in still greater obscurity. In all probability this question will never be settled—the learned and great have not been reluctant in expressing their convictions in favor of both positions. Among the variety of topics for speculation, none afford more ample scope than this. If the question could be decided, no very great conquest would be gained, nor would the species of the human race be much benefitted or edified by it.

The most plausible opinion, at first glance, would seem to be, that in proportion to the intelligence, is the happiness enjoyed—that importunities, bickerings, and strife recede before the lights of learning and wisdom, and that objects of smaller concern are forgotten in consequence of the mind being absorbed in subjects of greater magnitude, and of necessity deeper interest—that the higher order of intellects are capacitated to enjoy a higher de-

gree of felicity, by this assumption, than the less informed. If this were invariably true, a larger proportion of
the human race would be destitute of the means of happiness—their doleful lamentations would burthen the
winds with sighs, and the fair surface of the globe filied
with thorns of misery. In short, this Eden would be
converted into a Pandemonium—and the residence of
peaceful man into the habitations of the damned: for the
the larger portion of mankind are ignorant and illiterate.
If the position be correct, more attention would be paid
to the improvement of the sciences and arts—to the exaltation of human nature by means of such improvements, and the dissemination of truth, which renders human nature dignified—for all mankind should follow
those paths in which there are no thorns, and in which
are found the greater amount of uninterrupted happiness.

But it is generally believed that mankind are more frequently instruments of their own misfortunes than happiness. This would seem to militate against our thesis.
It does not, however, involve its correctness, for exceptions are found to all rules—it would not be a fair assumption to take a few isolated examples in confirmation
of this theory. It is not absurd to say that the more intelligence a man possesses the greater are his obligations,
and vice versa—following the rule inversely, that "where
little is given, little will be required."

Mr. Maddin, in his infirmities of Genius, has given the
characters of several men of eminence, before whose
mind's eyes appeared gorgeous visions and apparitions,
which created sensations of fear and of their having incur-
red the displeasure of their God. Cowper was a genius of
this description. Happiness had entirely forsaken his habi-

tations. Pleasure, with its fascinations, ceased to linger around him. Hope did not spring exultingly in his bosom, and these rendered his life a burthen to him. This example does not corroborate our theory, only so far as it shows how insusceptible men of learning generally are of the highest and sublimest enjoyments of life. It often blasts their reputations—it grieves them to see others apparantly in higher enjoyments than themselves. It was this reflection that brought heaviness and gloom upon the mind of Rasselas (one of Johnson's characters.) He beheld the beasts of the field more felicitous than himself. Clouds of grief hung thick around him—envy seized his heart and cloyed the vernal joys of life. But to reverse the picture, a quite different aspect is presented us. We behold pure, unadulterated, extatic happiness smiling around the abode of every man in ordinary circumstances. There peace uninterrupted reigns—there discord and contention seldom enter.

"The fond soul,
Wrapp'd in gay visions of unreal bliss,
Still paints the illusive form,"

is not applicable to his situation. The Savage life is the most happy, judging from external circumstances. The red man of the forest pursues such game as the country affords, and is satisfied. His bows and implements of sport are objects affording him exquisite amusement. He asks not for wealth and honors—but security in solitude. On public occasions these children of nature assemble together, animated with the prospective amusements which are to characterize the day. Unhallowed desires find no harbor in their bosoms. They celebrate the convival meeting with a rustic dance, and disperse in good humor.

Such a state of happiness the civilized community has never enjoyed: although civilized man would be unwilling to exchange his lot for that of the savage—the savage would be unwilling to make the exchange himself.

Alexander was not satisfied with the wealth and emoluments of a whole world, and Diogenes was content with the circumscribed limits of his tub. What induced this conqueror of the world to exclaim, "Were I not Alexander I would be Diogenes! It was the consciousness of his own misery when compared to the pleasures of Diogenes.

Upon the whole, I am rather inclined to the opinion that the more ignorant the man is the more happiness he enjoys: and on the contrary, that a man is better prepared to enjoy such happiness when his mental faculties are enlarged and expanded I will admit; but how often does he abuse it and heap ruin upon his own head. Surrounded as they were by all the glories of a Paradise, and instructed by the voice of the Deity, without having dreamed of bringing death into our world with all its woe, our First Parents were not contented—the tree of knowledge tempted them, and they ate of the forbidden fruit, and fell from their primeval simplicity and purity. And thus it is the world over. When a man is capable of enjoying himself he is not satisfied, and his changes are always for the worse.

AN ESSAY ON THE IMMORTALITY OF THE SOUL.

Upon no subject, probably within the range of human speculation has there been a greater diversity of opinion than the immortality of the soul. Some absolutely deny that there is such a thing. The doctrine of the immortality of the soul is not confined to the period of modern disputation alone, but it was strongly and ably advo· cated by ancient Sages and Philosophers, whose eyes never caught the light which the volume of Divine In· spiration has since spread over the world. This doctrine breathed from the inspired pen of Plato—it shed a hal· lowed light around the prison of Socrates—and it found an able defender in the person of the immortal Cicero. Minds that never read the sublime strains of Isaiah were convinced by the infallible evidences of human nature, and the demonstrations of science, that the grave did not complete their existence. It was the received notion that the soul had to cross the river Styx before it en· tered the abode of the blessed. The doctrine of metemp· sychosis propogated by the celebrated philosopher of Samos, discloses his belief, and that of the age generally, in which he flourished upon this point. The descent of Aleneas into the Infernal regions corroborates the same. But as the Christian Religion advances, this doctrine is more universally embraced, for upon this is it based.— How pleasing is the thought that our eternal existence does not terminate with this life; that our conditions will be generally improved, and that we will receive new accessions of happiness in every change, still approach· ing the perfections of the Deity? How it immeasura· bly expands the soul, exalts the mind, and incompara· bly magnifies our feelings and senses? The thought of death spreads a pall of gloom around us, and damps our spirits. But when we are convinced that the dead shall be raised again in newness of life—that that "which is sown in corruption shall be raised in incorruption—that which is sown in dishonor is raised in glory: in weakness raised in power—and that which is sown a natural body will be raised a spiritual body," our mourning is changed into superlative joy. What consolation can we lay to our bosom of the doctrine of Annihilationism be true? Upon what smoothe surface could we paint our objects of delight? Upon what beacon could our eyes rest, that would not soon be extinguished like a flickering taper? What desolate path would noble deeds and virtuous actions irradiate? In such belief is found

"No light; but rather darkness visible
Served only to discover sights of woe,
Regions of sorrow, doleful shades, where peace
And rest can never dwell."

Take away from man the hope of future enjoyments, and you virtually take from him every thing life is worth living for; you thereby stop up the fountain of bliss which flows from the throne of God to his creature man. Darkness would be his habitation on earth, and nonentity his portion when compelled to leave it. Upon this subject Cicero has expressed himself thus. "If I am wrong in believing that the souls of men are immortal, I please myself in my mistake; nor while I live will I ever choose that this opinion, with which I am so much delighted, should be wrested from me. But if, at death, I am to be annihilated, as some minute philosophers suppose, I am not afraid lest those wise men, when extinct too, should laugh at my error."

Apart from the lights of Revelation upon this subject, we are constrained by the dictates of reason and common sense to believe it. Annihilationism does not comport with the character, wisdom, and attributes of the Deity. It literally puts at naught the design of the Great Architect and Ruler of the Universe. It undermines the cardinal principles of the christian religion.—For if the soul be not immortal, I would not give a fig for the advantages of a Revelation. The loftiest aspirations of genius, the playful excursions of fancy, the unweaning desire of posthumous renown, the upspringing of elastic hope, the inward consciousness of good or bad actions, and the vaultings of a proud ambition afford ample indications of the existence of a principle that will never die.

"Whence springs this pleasing hope, this fond desire,
This longing after immortality?
Or, whence this secret dread, and inward horror,
Of falling into naught? Why shrinks the soul
Back on herself, and startles at destruction?"

has been asked by a man of high reputation, and in answer to his own question, solves the problem thus,

" 'Tis the divinity that stirs within us."

If death ends our existence, for what were we erected? Does man live merely to die? If so, what good has he accomplished by his death? Does a thirst for knowledge in its various departments—the certainty with which the revolutions of heavenly bodies have been computed—the celerity with which the ocean is fathomed and measured in search of the gems of priceless love, and the cupidity with which a discovery is siezed and communicated to the enlightened world, bear no evidence of man's immortal principles? Why erect those cloud-capt pyremids, those mausoleums and monumental piles. Those magnificent depositories of the immortal dead? Is it to perpetuate any event, or preserve in hallowed recollection the deeds and exploits of a favorite individual? What cares he for an honorable name to leave behind him if he is to sleep forever in the dark shades of oblivious night? Why leave a memorial of his greatness behind him?

"Who remembers not an hour of serious ecstasy when, perhaps, as he lay beneath some old tree and gazed on the setting sun, earth seemed a visionary thing, the glories of immortality were half revealed, and the first notes of universal harmony whispered to his soul? some moment, when he seemed almost to realize the eternal, and could have been well contented to yield up his mortal being? some little space, populous of high thoughts, and disinterested resolves—some touch upon that "line of limitless desires" along which he shall live in a purer sphere? [Unfinished.]

AN ESSAY ON THE CHARACTER OF MARTIN LUTHER.

With the Great Lutheran Reformation began an era in the world's history, rendered memorable by the triumph of truth and liberal opinions. Anterior to its commencement, all Europe was in a state of indescribable commotion. The clergy had usurped the civil authority, and fastened upon the people a spiritual Despotism. The elements of society were corrupt. Deluded by the Reverend Doctors of the Church, the people were made to believe that by a liberal contribution to the ecclesiastical treasury, the souls of departed friends and relatives would be released from purgatory, and wing their flight to heaven. If they cherished a parsimonious spirit, the souls of their loved ones would remain forever in the regions of the damned. This was the condition of Europe at the time that Luther appeared. Contrary to the wish of parents he entered the convent, and adhered devoutly to the Christian faith. He found his way into some library and discovered a book called the Bible. He opened it, and with many inconveniences he was finally enabled to read it. A flood of light bursted immediately across his understanding. He there inculcated the truth, that Religion could be obtained without money and without price. The seeds of corruption had ripened—the valcano was ready to burst. It was for Luther to contrive the safety-valves, and to still the elements in the end. In the language of a modern critic, "he came forth on the theatre of life another Sampson Agonistes, "with plain heroic magnitude of mind, and celestial vigor armed," ready to wage an unequal combat with the haughtiest of the giants of Gath; or to shake down, though it were on his own head, the columns of the proudest of her temples. He possessed no advantages resulting from a finished education; but he had a lion heart that knew no fear. It was not his purpose to overthrow the Church, nor to secede from it: his object was to correct its abuses. He openly and fearlessly met the learned Doctors of the Church in debate—refused to retract a single expression he had ever said or written, until he was convinced by demonstrative evidence that he had not truth for his support. They did not attempt to reason with him from scriptural data, for they were conscious they were in error—but by threats and demonstrations tried to awe him to submissiveness. This was an ineffectual way to induce such a man as Luther to renounce what he conceived to be true.

This was not a plausible course for those to pursue, whose object was to silence dispute. If men who hold to certain doctrines are satisfied they are in the right, they will fearlessly accept any challenge of investigation that may be offered. But unless they show by the unerring indications exhibited in their actions, that their cause has the semblance of truth, however credulous the adverse party may be, in many respects, they are nevertheless confirmed in the truthfulness of their own cause, and satisfied of weakness of their antagonist. Had the Catholics been willing to correct all flagrant abuses and corruptions existing—and they were certainly numerous—if they were actuated by that spirit which christianity breathes—it is not known what might have been the condition of the world at this day relative to its kind of religion. When we consider for a moment the Great Reformer, surrounded by those who threatened his dedestruction, and denounced him as a heretic, and that he voluntarily left Wittenburg, where he had a few adherents, Melancthon in their number, and went solitary and alone into a place in which he could expect no mercy from man, and after facing these dangers with an iron heart and trusting confidence in the Author of his faith, appearing before those who were to be his judges, with what feelings of deepest admiration for the man are we inspired? How magnanimous and yet how humble is his conduct? They imperiously, dogmatically and supercilliously command him to retract what he had previously said and written. He asks for an evidence of his having written or said anything that derogates from the character of the christian religion as revealed in the Bible. They again threaten and remonstrate, but truth is ever the same. With no other shield but this, he stands in their midst, nobly defying and begging them to meet him in a theological disputation. Tetzel's thunders were heard, but to no effect. His blows were warded off with admirable skill by Luther, who, but a man, was a giant when armed with truth.

If any thing of nobleness is attached to the hero of a romance, how doubly is it the case in Martin Luther, a real person divested of ficticious exaggeration, and who performed feats surpassed in intrepidity by no doughty knight known in the imaginations of men?

At this remarkable period, a spark was enkindled which now illumines millions of minds, otherwise doomed to be unknown to fame. By a remarkable coincidence, it has been said, Luther on the fourth of July, in a public disputation with his Popish antagonist at Leipsic, first called in question the divine right of the Pope.

That the spirit of free inquiry may continue to be unrestricted, and that evil may always find in some Modern Luther, a firm and uncompromising enemy, cannot, I am convinced, be too ardently hoped.

ESSAY ON THE CAPACITY OF THE PEOPLE FOR SELF GOVERNMENT.

Our subject for the deliberation of the day is one which, as I conceive, requires but little argument.— We are asked, are the people capable of self-government? I maintain that they are. Experience says they are.— History, though prolific with a delineation of fallen empires—of smoking ruins—of delapidated Cities—of mall administrations of government, tells us that a government solely in the hands of the people *en masse* is more likely to endure. When is a safer depository of power than in the hands of the sovereign people? Is it because they are ignorant, that they are incapable of self-government? If so, it is easy to find a remedy. Educate the people and they will evince to the world that they have minds that direct their decisions, and hearts that influence their motives. The bloody annals of the past have been spread out before us, presenting to the contemplative mind scenes terrific, and marches and countermarches, of Revolutions, of bloody battles, of "Gorgons and Chimeras dire," and of the instability of human institutions. Greece the cradle of the sciences and the arts, has been an exhaustless theme for the speculations of the philosopher and the declamation of the orator. Have they in general learned a moral from her picture? As prima facie evidence that man is incapable of self-government, we are told her institutions were founded upon the will of the sovereign people, and their wisdom was not sufficient to preserve even the very edifice which they themselves had been instrumental in creating. But let us calmly and dispassionately ask, was that nation of people ever free? Were they not slaves and mercenaries, whose good fortune had not been to be rich? Whilst they had freedom within the walls that surrounded them, their own brethren without were submitting to the galling yoke of oppression. Is it not so? History responds affirmatively.— What a Greek would call freedom, an American would call slavery. An opinion has prevailed, and has received the hearty sanction of the learned and great, that religion and freedom go hand in hand. Were the Greeks a religious people? Look at her brazen altars—the temples of her Gods—her marble monuments—her superstitious notions, and every thing derogatory to christianity. In the sublime conceptions of the deity they were heathens. Then we conclude they were never free—consequently never permitted to act and think for themselves. The reason they were incapable of self government is conclusive.

They were kept back in the dark. It was so at a still later period, even down to the 18th century, in almost every nation of Europe. They tacitly submitted to the rescripts and edicts of the Pope. Not one feebly, sickly ray of celestial light from the hallowed regions of Parnassus was permitted to dawn upon their understandings. They were kept in ignorance and barbarism, and a people unenlightened by the discoveries of science and inventions of art—unedified by the history of the past, which would have enabled them to prognosticate the future—untutored in lessons of moral instructions and religion, can never act with discretion. The Pope of Rome is not ignorant of this, and uses all his influence to keep the people from open day. We should never take the history of a nation of people who were emersed in ignorance and confined in darkness, and draw a conclusion from the fate of that people, that other nations whose minds are cultivated by the plowshare of knowledge, whose manners are civilized, whose hearts are influenced by the principles which the Bible inculcates, and whose iron-hearted valor enables them to stand firm by their proud eagle and their glorious constitution will inevitably share the same fate. Enlightened with knowledge, people become giants, they burst the chains which bind them to the dust, and a flashing torrent of celestial day bursts through the shadowy void which ignorance had created. They are now prepared to act for themselves. They, no more like serfs, follow the charriot wheels of some darring military chieftain to the field of conquest and dessolation. But the question as propounded to us, does not confine us to the capacities the people have to regulate finances, make and abolish laws, and other correlative terms. We are inquiring are the people capable of self government? Self preservation is the first law of Nature. But we will not do the gentlemen advocating the opposite side of this question the injustice to present it under this distorted appearance, believing that the question was only intended to embrace the capabilities of the multitude. If however we can succeed in proving by logical principles, that man in all ages of the world is and has been fully qualified to preserve, protect and defend himself—if this principle be exemplified in the inhabitants of the arid climes of Africa—if the unlettered savage, roaming in the solemn primeval forest, where the axe of civilization was never heard, embraces all the faculties which enable him to shelter himself from the pelting storm—defend his rights—his home—his country—his all—at the hazzard of loosing his life, we can settle the question without a doubt, that the people who have made themselves intelligent, are alway scompetent to do—to act correctly without danger to themselves or their country. This is so plain that none pretend to deny it. We are taught that union is strength, that it is the palladium upon which the dearest interests of society rest.

Keeping this directly before us, remembering what man individually can accomplish unassisted by others, collecting themselves together from the various parts of the world, and entering into a social compact or agreement, we are unhesitatingly constrained to declare that our position is true—for union is strength, and a collection or society of men, by the aid of their judgments, can unquestionably effect more than one man could dream of effecting. But more serious considerations invite our attention. Lafayette speaking in reference to France says, "for a nation to be free it is sufficient that she wills it." This cannot be controverted or misunderstood . There must be volition before an act. The people should believe they are fully competent to discharge the functions of government. This is not a subject difficult of comprehension. It has none of those secret windings of the labyrinth by which it is hard to get a "clew" at it—none of those enigmas which puzzle the mind to unriddle. "Government," says Swift, "is a plain thing, and fitted to the capacity of many heads." Altho' every individual is not expected to make this his study, there are enough in all governments who qualify themselves for it, and who advocate its measures. Because we are not all preachers it is no reason that we cannot be christians. Because all are not professedly financiers and practical statesmen, we are not to infer that the people are ignorant of what is their interest and enjoyment. . Few such geniuses as Milton and Shakspeare have ever lived, but we cannot say the world has no taste for poetry, and no genius to write it. Though they may not be able to write any thing equal to them, they know well enough what it takes to constitute a poet, and when his writings and verses are defective. Though we are not all statesmen, we know when the wheels of government are clogged, and every patriot is found exerting his power to regulate them.— Government has been considered by many, especially those opposed to republican principles, as a mere experimental machine, that no sooner has the experiment been made a change is suggested, and 'change is not reform, and the freedom which that administration of government afforded would be entombed never to be resuscitated or reanimated. If it perish, the wisdom or folly which framed it must perish also. But who is it that are instrumental in effecting these changes which end in explosion of public sentiment, which

"Like bubbles on the sea of matter borne,
They rise they break, and to that sea return."

Some designing knave or ranting politician who, preventing the people being enlightened by witholding from their
eyes the lights of truth, succeeds in enlisting the people
in his favor, and he proudly tramples up the gorgeous
ruins. Not because they had not judgment of their
own, but because they were constrained to go for the
measure right wor rong. They were not induced to sustain those measures from choice or desire. In short, they
had no voice in the matter. Reason was offered them,
but not with winning words they conquered willing hearts,
and made persuasion do the work of fear. We are too
apt to be blinded and deceived by names. We are not
unfrequently told the people are the sovereign rulers,
when they have no direct voice in the matter. England,
for instance, may have so considered herself in the time
of Oliver Cromwell. The parliament which had been
so omnipotent, refused to act in accordance with the wishes of Cromwell, and with speedy vengeance and vindic-
tive spleen, he desolved the long Rump Parliament.—
And yet it is said the people had a voice in the matter,
but like Stentor, his voice thundered louder than all. It
is so in other instances. The people are said to be govern-
ors, when they themselves are ruled as with a rod of iron.
And because the government is either destroyed or cor-
rupted, it is inferred the people are incapable of self government. We should lay aside such false reasoning.—
Let us take a nation for example, where the people are,
in truth and in fact, the rulers; where no dread deters
them from an open, honest, sacred, discharge of their
imperative duty. We may look abroad to other nations
but they are still in ignorance. Its Cimmerian mantle

is thrown over them, and some protuberent Teneriffe has intercepted the rays of moral, religious light, that was about to dawn upon their minds. No rain-bow of promise is painted on the dark clouds of their destiny; for their hands are yet tied. Spain has no voice in the matter, and silence broods over her domain. Ireland is not heard, for she too is tongue-tied. Italy is mute. South America has sealed her lips hermetically. France, like a ghost, does not speak at all. England has been stammering and throwing out her parrot-articulation, but she is not understood. Our own country, with her eagle glory––her unrivalled freedom and independence––her enlightened citizens and patriotic warriors––her orators, statesmen and divines––her commerce and her manufactures––her Literary Institutions, like our own lovers of wisdom, alone has a voice in this great decision. We heard her first signal at Lexington––we heard her groaning at Camden, and then cheering at the top of her voice ––triumphant cheers proceed from the plains of Saratoga––thundering shouts of triumph and victory passed along her lines at Trenton, and ceased not to be heard at Yorktown. 'Twas the people who rose in the majesty of their strength, "and asserted to the world they would be free, and struck the blow that gave her liberty.

ESSAY ON WESTERN LITERATURE.

More has been done within the last half century towards the dissemination of useful knowledg among the people, than the most sanguine could have anticipated, in view of the period just preceding it. The stimulants to enterprise which are incident to a nation where knowledge, like virtue, have has its own reward, contribute essentially to the advancement of the cause of letters. It is because of an honorable competition between hopeful aspirants to distinction and renown. It results from the fact that no empire, save that of the mind, is recognised; and over this the assiduous and untiring are generally the sole monarchs. The marvelous and astonishing inventions of the age attest, in part, a high degree of enlightenment of public sentiment.

Improvements in the mechanic arts are marching onward with a pace hitherto unequalled in our history—the most distant parts of our country have, in a manner, been rendered contiguous by the unparalleled rapidity of conveyance and communication, which unites the citizen of the frozen north with the citizen of the sunny south, in a community of feeling and interest—preparations for war, offensive and defensive, are being made in accordance with the injunction left us by the Father of his country, which places the United States in an independent attitude to the belligerant powers of the world—facilities for development of mind, the home of the Deity, are daily enlarging and extending alike to the rich and the poor—the majesty of the American Laws and Institutions is respected and acknowledged throughout our limits——and a Commerce freighted with the richest products of a virgin soil, spreads her sails upon every ocean. All these conspire to render this country eminently and unquestionably superior to any other, as they are conducive to a freedom of thought and independence of character, the exercises of which are measurably forbidden in the monarchies of the Old World. Although much may be said in commendation of the wholesome influence of our Government, and the innumerable advantages which spring up spontaneously on every hand, to elevate and dignify the American character, it cannot be disguised, that the means to effect such desirable ends have been left unemployed. In short, we are far from having attained an Augustan age in our Literature, or even to that state of improvement and exaltation that hope had pictured.— What then are the influences which have contributed to retard the march of mind? What Burkley has attempted to check its progress by boisterously declaring that "learning has brought disobedience, and heresy, and sects into the world, and printing has divulged them, and libels against the best Government?" The question is easily settled, if we regard the signs of the times as the true index. There may be various causes, or combination of causes, which have a salutary effect in stopping the onward, progressive movements that have been going on in the intellectual world. But no one thing of which we are acquainted, has had a greater agency and more powerful influence in producing such a result, than that almost universally prevalent rage of utilitarianism which has enlisted in its favor too many idolatrous votaries. A spirit of economy cannot receive too great encouragement, if it does not transcend its proper limits into parsimoniousness. Truly is the love of money the root of all evil when applied to the case before us; for any thing may be regarded as an evil that contributes, though in the smallest degree, to check those means which are the prime sources of wealth, whilst they incomparably enhance the general happiness, and elevate and dignify the human character. To gratify this sorded passion, the most imminent perils have been braved.— Mankind too generally dream of the gold of Ophir, and the invaluable gems in the imaginary regions of El-Dorado! The riches of Crœsus and Astor are of a greater desideratum than the immortality of Shakspeare and Milton. The classic grounds of antiquity, and the hill of science fade from memory's tablet when fortune smiles. Unlike the historian of Halicarnassus, who visited the countries of Greece, Thrace, Scythia, Mesapotamia, Syria, and Egypt, in quest of that information which has handed his name down to the courts of Prince Posterity, to whom Dean Swift has dedicated one of his epistles, few are disposed to devote a modicum of their time and talents to the advancement of learning unrequited.

Men of gifted intellects and towering geniuses have been induced to forsake the Muse of Poetry, Romance and History, to pursue those airy phantoms at which the unlettered world is grasping with the most astonishing avidity. Youths whose hopes are bright, and aspirations lofty, are circumscribed in the sphere of usefulness, by the notion that some parents fondly cherish, that wealth is the only road to distinction. In this opinion they not unfrequently neglect the proper mental training that is necessary to secure to the son a fair standing in society, which obliges him, imperatively, to follow where he might have led, and feel his own inferiority where he might have ruled. This is in consequence of that self-aggrandizing spirit which we have been deprecating. May we not anticipate a time when a more glorious era shall illumine our history—when a deeper interest is aroused among the people upon the subject of education—and when the whole country shall smile under one continual blaze of improvement? By a slight reformation in public opinion, which is the great lever by which good or evil is produced, and the influence of judicious laws, the golden visions of the theorist and enthusiast may be realized. The Eastern part of our country is generally regarded as superior to the Western, in the facilities of improvement which she affords. It is because she has a larger population to the extent of territory, and because she has been longer settled. She is consequently more able to support literary institutions than a country newly settled. But as the older States of the Union are becoming crowded by the natural increase of our species, a new field of enterprise invites them to the West. Like De Sota in quest of riches, or like Juan Ponce de Leon in search of the fabled fountain of perpetual youth, they penetrate the bosom of its "solemn, primeval forest." The tide of emigration is swelling, and rapidly rolling on to the place where its proud waves are to be stayed. It may be said with more than poetical justice that

"Westward the star of empire takes its way."

The wilderness is beginning to blossom as a rose, under the influence of seasonable cultivation. Magnificent edifices of more than Medicean splendor are raising their heads in unsullied grandeur to the skies. In this auspicious state of things shall the lamp of knowledge. that was lit upon the altar of liberty be extinguished? Are there no Mæcenases to patronize and encourage an indigenous literature? To this end there must needs be a regular system of communication—a mutual, liberal interchange of thought among the people, without which the general information would unavoidably be very limited. The press is the great luminary from which the rays of intellectual light are to eminate. As the stars in the firmament effect the night, so do the printing presses effect the night of ignorance that hangs over a nation.— Shall the West be deprived of one of these stars that diffuse light abroad? May a Literary Journal or Review not be established in Nashville, that will vie in literary merit with the most extensively circulated periodical in the Union? There is nothing to prevent it but a want of pecuniary means. It is highly discreditable to the West that such laudable enterprises have not hitherto met with more general encouragement. It is mostly attributed to that false-directed zeal, which we have seen, transcends all others in the pursuit of its object. It is certainly for no want of talent, that we have not long since been edified and delighted by such a journal, for we can unpresumptuously boast of as able writers as those who contribute to the Literary Periodicals of the East. Such a project in successful operation would much improve the immorality of the people, to which they have a remarkable proclivity, provided it be conducted in that way as to deserve the most liberal patronage. The tone of its morals should be elevated—lofty—pure. The spirit that it breathes should be unbought, unsaleable, and uncorrupted patriotism.

AN ESSAY ON AMBITION.

There is a passion that rankles in the human breast which is highly necessary to enable the individual to meet and overcome difficulties, but supremely pernicious if permitted to go unrestrained. It is known by the name of ambition. There are many, it must be remembered, who are vastly deficient in such a spirit which prompts to manly exertion and laudable enterprises; but there are others who rush thoughtlessly and precipitately into the most imminent danger, without any prospective means of getting out. The absence of it in the one is as much to be regretted, as the excess in the other is to be commiserated. There is a latent fire in the bosom of some, which we seldom observe unless by very faint emissions, or when the subject is agitated by a great momentous occasion, the slumbering fire is enkindled and glows with unusual fervour. In some we find it over-flowing, and as redundant as the waters of Arethusa.— Over their actions it has complete and decided mastery. It is a great and powerful incentive to action. It prompts to the discharge of duty, and not unfrequently to acts of supererogation. The individual forgets the propriety of pursuing a course "in medies rebus," and like the ill-fated Icarus, soars too lofty in the presumptuousness of enthusiastic youth, and his pinions of wax are melted, and his sanguine ardor damped. This runs thoughout our whole nature: it insinuates itself into every circumstance in life. In some it is the brightest jewel in their char-acter: in others it is "like the toad, ugly and venom-ous." The one we praise: the other we despise. The patient enquirer after truth for its own sake, elicits our approbation, and that of every lover of wisdom. His aspirations are above the common pursuits of life. He desires, it is true, to deserve the confidence and esteem of mankind, but he is unwilling to pay too extravagant a price for it. The approbation of one's conscience is really worth more than the applause of men and their 'fawning sycophancy.' He emulates to excel, not to put others down. He wishes to rise, but not on the injured reputation of another. Love of country finds an abode in his affections. The pleasing ambition of defending her insulted rights and liberties burns, like Ætna in his bosom, though not suffered to burst forth to corrode and destroy. No promise of exaltation or favor can inḋuce him to become recreant to her interest. He be-- comes her oracle and champion. His voice is heard; when necessary, in defence of civil and religious freedom. Of such men are the Hampdens, the Sydneys, the Miltons, the Washingtons and the Franklins, who contended for these principles so earnestly and vehemently, that posterity rises up and calls them blessed. Those who first sowed the seminal principes of Reform, that Nations, might be free, are truly entitled to our gratitude. It was for no conceivable pecuniary or e lesiastical distinction that induced Luther, the lion of reformation, or as he has been more appropriately termed, the "Christian Hercules, the heroic cleanser of the Augean stables of Apostacy," with his learned friend and coadjutor, Melancthon' and others, to nullify the edicts of the Pope, and shake Papacy to the centre throughout all Christendom by the native force of their intellects. They contended for a spiritual disenthraldom, and to disrobe the Pope of that authority which he had so unconscientiously abused.— Nor did they abuse the power which they had gained.— They possessed zeal worthy of the men, and as such it should be cherished and cultivated. If it is shamefully abused, the individual had better never have been bern.. Who can estimate the injury done the world, morally, ecclesiastically and politically by the perversion of intel- lect? Can it be calculated how much evil has been done by the subtle and insidious talent of Gibbon upon Christianity—the incredulity of Hume—the sarcastic and venomous sneers of Voltaire—the infidel deism of Rousseau, and the stubborn impiety and low ribaldry of Paine? Had their minds been directed towards the proper objects, they might justly have been called the benefactors, instead of the enemies of mankind. The shock that has been given to religion by such men will be felt many days hence. It is hard to eradicate entirely from the mind, long existing errors. No truth is more evident than that "the evil a man does lives after him." The influence of example is great and salutary. It lives after the man has passed the cold Jourdan of death. Like the setting of the sun in the West, leaving a radiance and lustre behind, the character and disposition of an individual will remain after he is dead, and have an influence upon those with whom he lived and associated.

There is another category of men entitled to but little of our gratitude or commendation. If the warrior, eager for battle, and animated by a spirit of liberty, perishes around her sacred temple, he is engaged in a good cause, and we lament his fall. If by his dauntless Herculean bravery he protects it from violence, we join in exultation, and admire his zeal. But when oceans of blood have been shed, and human victims bleed at her shrine in resisting oppression—when iron-heeled despotism struts through the land, nations weep and tremble. The earth we tread is one common battlefield. War is the study of the wise, and work of the brave. The conqueror secures his victory and prepares for new conquest.—He slays the last enemy, and weeps for more worlds to conquer. The world seems too little for him, when at the same time, a philosopher had "ample room and verge enough" in a tub.

The lion of Carthage whose ambition led him to think he could conquer the proud mistress of the world, died an ignoble death before he had released himself from his allegiance. The man of Corsica breathed his last a miserable exile at St. Helena. Ill-fated ambition destroys their aspirations, and most all the conquerors in the annals of history, who fought for plunder, rapine and power in the end, had to submit to, and be contented with the victory of *Pyrrhas*.

AN ESSAY ON THE CHIVALRY OF TENNESSEE.

Ever since Tennessee made her advent into the Union as a State, her history has been replete with the most illustrious daring of her citizens. There never was a time when she failed to contribute her aid in the defence of the Union. Invincibility has been written on the escutcheon of her military renown. Whenever a position of the enemy is to be moved, her pennant is always seen waving above the breach. In the last war with Great Britain, in which she rendered herself signally illustrious, she evinced a patriotism and a chivalry which challenges the admiration of the world. She met and repelled a magnanimous and hitherto invincible soldiery. The pride and boast of the British Nation who had defeated Napoleon at the battle of Waterloo, who were led to the charge by a brave commander, had to cower before the dauntless Tennesseans. Napoleon who waved his victorious flag, nearly, throughout all Europe, and who, in other words, stretched his subduing "arm over Egypt and the Isles, until Arab and Ethiopia bowed in bondage, and the triumphs of Alexander became the trophies of the modern Hercules," was signally defeated by the Duke of Wellington at the battle of Waterloo. The flower of his army flushed with victory gained over the French, led the van at the battle of New Orleans. The result of the engagement is well known. Tennessee soldiers, commanded by a Tennessee General, rebuked the insolence of the invaders in the most summary manner, as you well know. This gives her a supremacy over all

O

our citizens, and raise, upon one or two occasions, the shout of victory, but like the last song of the swan, it will be but the premonitor of their early defeat.

Suppose it were possible upon this occasion that we were placed in one vast amphitheatre of Nature, and suppose that upon consulting about what course to pursue in relation to the war, the ghosts of our revolutionary ancestors were to appear in the galleries, where they could be spectators of what was said or done? Suppose it possible with their gastly looks to participate in our councils, what would be their language of admonition and encouragement? The Father of his country would tell us that as we had prepared for war in time of peace, to live independent or sink in the grave; the dauntless Warren, who was an early martyr in the cause of human liberty, would say as he perished in his youth, let the youth grasp his sword for the combat, and cut the gordian knot of oppression or perish amid the din of arms.

Another would exhort us as we love our country and her institutions, "don't give up the ship."

Another who had "filled the measure of his country's glory" would tell us now is the golden moment to move; to let action be our motto, and "all is safe." Who that has the heart of a patriot within his bosom would be insensible to their admonition? Who would not respond, that as he loves his country—as he is proud that he is an American citizen, as he reveres the sacred ashes of his fathers, he is willing to fight, and if he falls, the cause of liberty will not fall with him?

THE END.

Lightning Source UK Ltd.
Milton Keynes UK
UKHW010610120219
337137UK00007B/1440/P